D0490526

With the Argylls

With the
Argylls

A Soldier's Memoir
Ray Ward

Edited by Robin Ward

Foreword by Trevor Royle

BIRLINN

Published in 2014 by Birlinn, West Newington House, 10 Newington Road
Edinburgh EH9 1QS www.birlinn.co.uk

First published as *The Mirror of Monte Cavallara*. Birlinn 2006

Copyright © the Estate of Ray Ward 2014

Foreword © copyright Trevor Royle 2014

Afterword © copyright Robin Ward 2014

ISBN 978 1 84341 066 9

British Library Cataloguing-in-Publication Data. A catalogue record for
this book is available from the British Library

Typeset in Minion and Myriad by Robin Ward

Printed and bound in Italy by Grafica Veneta www.graficaveneta.com

Contents

Dedicated to my sons
Robin and Brian
and to the memory of
my fellow Argylls

Foreword

To gain some understanding of what a soldier feels like before going into battle it is only necessary to read Ray Ward's account of an action in Italy in October 1944 which saw British infantrymen attacking a heavily defended German position on Monte Cavallara. At the time he was commanding a rifle company in 1st Battalion The Argyll and Sutherland Highlanders during the long and frequently bitter assault which took the Allied armies up through Italy towards the Gothic Line, the formidable German redoubt which ran from La Spezia in the west to Pesaro in the east and which made good use of the unbroken line of the Apennine mountain range. The task fell to A Company and the orders received by Ward were unambiguous. It was vital, said the commanding officer, that the position be taken 'at all costs'. In other words the men of the Argylls had to press home their attack regardless of casualties and that is precisely what they did. At dawn on 7 October 1944 the attack went in as planned but all too soon A Company was in trouble as it ran into sustained German machine-gun and mortar fire. Reinforcements arrived in the shape of B Company and eventually the position was captured but at some cost. All told, the Argylls lost 15 men killed and 44 wounded—30 percent casualties. Later, Ward reflected that it had not been 'a big show, just a routine attack with a limited objective; wishful thinking by the brass to seek a breakthrough then in that part of the line'.

In the wider history of the Italian campaign Monte Cavallara was probably little more than a footnote but at the time it was a sobering reminder of the price which must be paid by a thin screen of infantry ordered to attack a heavily defended position to prevent the wider advance stalling. However, behind that bleak arithmetic of war Ward tells another story describing the kind of men who went into the attack and delineating their hopes and fears. It soon becomes clear that it was not all derring-do and happy warriors. Amongst his three platoon commanders was a newly arrived subaltern who admitted his fears and thought he would not survive the battle, thereby breaking a taboo amongst men in the front line. Sadly, it turned out to be a self-fulfilling prophecy. Another officer died in agony, his 'mangled guts spilling out on the ground' as Ward tried to comfort him with a tot of rum. During the fighting a reluctant sergeant could not hide his relief when a bullet hit him in the foot, thereby providing him with a legitimate passport out of battle. Then, in the second wave Ward witnessed his fellow company commander kicking some of his men who had seen the killing power of the German spandau machine-guns and were not exactly keen to go over the top. None of this is related in a critical way but it is telling. By that stage of the war Ward was an experienced soldier who had seen sights no humans should be permitted to see and his words are a reminder that in the hellish fear of battle men sometimes forget to die like heroes. It is small wonder that his sons remember that their father was plagued by flashbacks and nightmares from that period in his life, probably suffering from what we now know to be posttraumatic stress disorder.

In that sense, these memoirs bear witness to a conflict which has become almost unimaginable for later generations. Written in retirement and based on his wartime diaries Ward's reminiscences are at once candid, revealing and deeply human; they are the real stuff of history. They give a wonderful insight into the impulses that drove young men in 1939 and 1940 to address the unfinished business of the earlier global conflict. Thomas Raymond Ward was far from being an unwilling conscript and during his basic infantry training he emerged not only as a natural soldier but at an early stage showed that he was 'officer material': the encomium came from a prewar regular sergeant with experience of service in China and India's North-west Frontier—a good judge. Posted to an Officer Cadet Training Unit, Ward continued to make good progress as the large and frequently unwieldy wartime army began to take shape.

In many respects it was the nation in uniform, a huge melting pot in which youngsters came from every kind of background, having been thrown together to do their bit for king and country. In general they were malleable and reasonably willing soldiers. Most did not fight for well-defined abstracts such as duty and honour although it was not difficult to uncover a deep seated and genuine belief that Nazism was evil and had to be crushed. Above all, a quest for adventure played a part and it was never far away from Ward's mind especially when he found that his battalion was bound for service in North Africa. At a time when the majority of the British population did not have access to foreign travel and cheap package holidays belonged to the distant future the chance to travel was a huge spur and one which most recruits embraced even though service overseas brought with it the possibility of seeing action. After all these were young men who believed that death happened to other people and that with luck they would emerge from the fighting unscathed.

Added to that heady optimism which has always encouraged young men to place themselves in danger there was also the certain knowledge that for most of them the war was finite, that they had signed up for the duration and that there had to be something better in store once the guns had finally fallen silent. In no other episode is this belief more tellingly exposed than in Ward's observation about the treatment of soldiers aboard the troopship taking them to Egypt by way of the long route around South Africa. Whereas the officers enjoyed peacetime standards of cruise ship comfort, the soldiers occupied cramped and fetid quarters below decks. While this did not turn Ward into a socialist overnight he remained convinced that treatment of that kind must have influenced returning servicemen to vote Labour in the first postwar General Election in the summer of 1945.

Once in North Africa the 1st Argylls became part of the Eighth Army, the great desert force which defeated the German and Italian armies in 1942 and in so doing gave the first signs of hope that the war could be won. In common with other soldiers who served in North Africa Ward was enormously impressed by the wild beauty of his surroundings which had few comparisons with any other theatre of the Second World War. At first acquaintance the North African terrain was harsh, barren and inhospitable, but it was also strangely compelling, a landscape which imprinted itself on the minds of the men who fought there. In fact, very few failed to be affected by the sheer size of the desert arena over which the two opposing armies fought and noted with approval its absence of definition and the seemingly limitless horizons with few roads or tracks to break up the bare expanse of sand and scrub. Responding to its similarities with a classical sporting arena, war correspondents on both sides tended to report the conflict using an imagery which spoke of a courtly tournament involving valiant rivals and chivalrous generals. Ward, too, seems to have been similarly enraptured and his response was probably influenced by the fact that part of his service in the desert saw his platoon acting as headquarters bodyguard to the eccentric but gifted General Bernard Law Montgomery who was admired by his men because he was obviously a winner yet was cautious of their lives.

Memoirs of this kind are one of the means in which later generations gain their understanding of past conflicts and in that respect Ward does not disappoint. Unlike volumes based on the recording of veterans' memories which became such a standby of military historiography in the later part of the twentieth century, and in so doing frequently distorted past events by seeing them through the prism of the present, Ward's reminiscences have the freshness of being based on words that were written at the time. It's the old story: the closer the writer is to events the better chance the reader has of being able to understand them. Read in that unforgiving light *With the Argylls* passes a vital test. Not only is it a classic in its own right but it can happily take its place alongside other luminous works of literature from the same conflict such as Peter Cochrane's *Charlie Company* and Martin Lindsay's *So Few Got Through*, both of which describe the dirty business of war from the point of view of a junior but thoroughly engaged infantry officer. It really is as good as that.

Trevor Royle
Edinburgh, Spring 2014

1 The Castle

My call up papers arrived in March 1940. I reported for an interview and army medical at Whiteinch recruiting office, a wooden hut on Dumbarton Road in Glasgow. The process was rather casual, like the Phoney War of the time. There had been no significant action in Western Europe since Nazi Germany invaded Poland on 3 September 1939, and no jingoistic rush to the recruiting offices at the start of the War as there had been in 1914. The interview was with a whiskery First World War veteran who confirmed my place and date of birth: Glasgow, 18 November 1916. I was 23 years old. He passed me as fit and asked which branch of the services I wanted to join. He almost had me down for the navy because my father, Alexander Ward, had been military bandmaster on the *Empress*, a cadet training ship on the Clyde. I chose the army, the infantry, preferably the Argylls. The Regiment was based at Stirling Castle, near the battlefields of Wallace, Bruce and Bonnie Prince Charlie whose exploits I had been taught at school and had read about in the novels of Buchan, Stevenson and Scott. I fancied the ceremonial uniform with its kilt bristling with a badger-head sporran, its wildcat and boar's head regimental badge and its chequered glengarry. The Argylls recruited from my part of the country, so my request was granted.

On 18 April 1940 I travelled by bus with a group of young conscripts to Stirling. Its streets were full of soldiers: squads of men marching here and there; off-duty officers and men walking about saluting each other right and left; military vehicles aplenty. It was a garrison town and this was wartime. Its castle is perched on the crest of an ancient volcanic crag and the walk to it on cobbled streets is a long one, uphill all the way. We were a ragged outfit of all shapes and sizes and all manner of dress, all of us variously fearful, resentful, resigned or bewildered. The only thing we had in common was our youth and an acceptance of our duty to serve our country and do our bit, like the men of the previous generation.

I recall the curious allure of Armistice Day when all the staff where I had worked, as a clerk in the office of a construction firm, John Train and Company, opposite the City Chambers in George Square, would gather at the windows overlooking the Cenotaph and see the vast crowd, bare-headed and motionless for the two minute's silence. Then a bugler would sound the 'Last Post' followed by beating drums, the skirl of the pipes and the swagger of kilted soldiers in the March Past which closed the ceremony. I had left school at sixteen at a time when many were out of work (as my father had been periodically) and there was much poverty, and was fortunate with a white-collar job. Nevertheless, military service offered an escape. I was physically fit and I looked forward to an adventure: to being a soldier, performing heroic deeds, winning military glory and all that.

Boys and young men in those days had their imagination stirred by stories of wartime heroism in books and films and by middle-aged veterans with tales to tell. I recall two old soldiers in the office. One was the senior clerk whose clearest memory of the Salonika campaign was of a troop train full of bayonet-brandishing soldiers inflamed by alcohol fighting among themselves. He would regale the office juniors with a blow-by-blow account of the brawl, which he told as a warning against the evils of strong drink bringing out the violent streak in men. We were suitably impressed since we knew nothing of strong drink and the only violence any of us had seen was on the school playground. The other veteran was the foreman joiner whose enormous, calloused left hand was minus two fingers. With grim relish he would tell how that very hand, after having been mauled by a piece of shrapnel from a German artillery shell one day in Flanders, had been thrust into a bucket of boiling tar to cauterise the wound.

We emerged from Stirling town onto the Castle Esplanade, a wind-swept parade ground we would come to know well. At its far end were the castle's ramparts, turrets and crow-step gables. A wooden drawbridge was flanked by two sentry boxes. Neither sentry deigned to give us even a glance. We crossed the bridge and approached the massive sixteenth-century Gatehouse where we got a foretaste of what was in store. We were stopped in our tracks by our first army command and challenge: 'Halt! Where do you miserable lot think you're going?'

The roar of sergeant-majors, the parade ground stamp of drilling troops, the rattle of musketry, the skirl of the pipes and the bugle calls that divide a soldier's day have echoed over Stirling's rooftops for over 200 years. In 1794 the Duke of Argyll raised the 91st Argyllshire Highlanders, recruiting men mainly from Glasgow and the west of Scotland; the 93rd Sutherland Highlanders was raised in 1799, from the Countess of Sutherland's militia and crofters. In 1881 the 91st and 93rd merged as The Argyll and Sutherland Highlanders, 1st and 2nd battalions respectively. Stirling Castle became the Regimental Depot. In 1940 it was the Infantry Training Centre.

When the 93rd was raised each man was invited to step forward for a customary dram with Major General Wemyss, cousin of the countess. That was the only formality. There was no whisky with the castle's commanding officer for us. Instead, we lost our civilian identity in an army number and our hair in a brutal cut. Next we got our kit: boots, battle-dress, balmoral; mess tin, enamel mug, cutlery; sewing and shaving kit, and brushes and polish for buttons, badges and boots. Later, we were each issued with a service rifle, ammunition clips, bayonet, steel helmet, gas mask and an anti-mustard gas oilskin cape. The weight of all this gear was about 50 pounds. None of the items had changed much since the First World War.

The sergeant at the Gatehouse had directed us across the cobbles to our quarters in the Top Square, the upper courtyard. Most recruits at the castle were housed in the sixteenth-century Great Hall, once the Stewart kings' ceremonial and banqueting chamber. This sounded grand until you went inside. The vast space had been filled with three floors of spartan accommodation, to billet soldiers sent north to subdue and punish the Jacobites after the rising of 1745. Our barrack was in the adjacent Chapel Royal, another venerable building which had been adapted crudely by the army. This was where we were thrown together before Lights Out that first night and where I got to know my fellow conscripts. They were from

Stirling and its hinterland, Glasgow and Clydeside, west-coast towns and the crofts of Argyll. Some fellows were hardy country lads. Most were city boys, many in poor physical shape, some from slums. We were split up into squads named after regimental battle honours: Corunna, Lucknow, Balaclava, Mons. I was pleased to find myself in Balaclava Squad, as I had thrilled as a boy to the story of the Thin Red Line when the 93rd repulsed a Russian cavalry charge during the Crimean War.

Each day began with Reveille at 0600 hours to shouts of 'Shake a leg!' from our non-commissioned officers (NCOs). They were our instructors and were feared and respected, demanding instant obedience always. We stumbled out of our beds into sandshoes, singlet and shorts. Then we were turfed outside for 45 minutes of physical training in the cold dawn air. We shaved, washed and dressed for breakfast which was taken in the Palace Block, the old royal apartments. Our mess hall and kitchen were on the lowest floor, formerly King James V's pantry and wine cellar. What wine there was now was out of bounds in the Officers' Mess, located in the former royal courtiers' and castle governors' chambers above us. That was a source of sardonic interest. So was the food, although some recruits thought it was better than they got at home.

One of the first things we were taught was how to stand properly to attention and salute smartly. Drill was deafening. The words came rattling out through the drill sergeant's teeth like machine-gun fire: 'Eyes to the front. From the right, quick march. Left, right, left, right. Swing those arms. Squad, halt!' We birled around in our new boots, trying not to slip on the cobbles or bump into each other. Anyone larking around was made to quick march around the square while the rest of us watched. I was the tallest man in the squad. I wore my balmoral in the most acceptable manner, got a good shine on my boots and polish in my cap badge. One morning I was praised as 'the only man in this bloody squad who knows how to wear an 'effing balmoral' and appointed right marker: the first to take up position in the Top Square whenever the squad paraded, and on whom the front rank formed up. The sergeant knocked us into such good shape that Balaclava Squad was named the best-drilled in the class, able to parade smartly in platoons of 30 or companies of 100 men.

After breakfast I often slipped off with my mug of tea to enjoy a first cigarette of the day (almost everybody smoked in those days, especially soldiers). I had discovered a quiet spot above the south ramparts with a panoramic view: to the south the Church of the Holy Rude and the pantiled rooftops of the town; to the west a spread of open country and the distant mountains of Argyll. It was my only chance in the day for a moment's solitude. Time up, I would toss the tea leaves down the side of the escarpment and send the fag end spinning through the air before dashing over the cobbles of the Top Square to prepare for the 0800 parade and the sergeant's shout, 'Right marker'.

We attended lectures on military history, infantry tactics and weapons, care of kit and hygiene. Each of us took a turn as barrack room orderly, floor scrubbing and tidying up while the squad was being harried about elsewhere. Each week, at the squad sergeant's command 'Stand by your beds', every item of our bedding, clothing and equipment was displayed for inspection. Any flaw exposed by the army's fetish for scrutiny and cleanliness usually provoked a verbal assault and a charge, which meant three days confined to barracks and menial tasks. There was little time to grumble about having our lives disrupted by the restrictions on our freedom and the demand for unquestioning obedience; by being shouted at all day, by the lack of home comforts and privacy, by the loss of personal identity in the military machine. Such time off as we got was spent in a canteen and recreation room run by the padre who was liked and respected by the recruits for his encouragement, advice and help solving personal problems. I had no inkling that wartime service would take a big slice out of my life. That's what happened to a whole generation of young people then. Generally biddable, we were not given to questioning authority, the established social order or the imperial certainties of the time.

We were marched across the drawbridge to the Esplanade many times as the months passed, on our way to and from church parades, route marches and weapons and battle training. We drilled for battlefield formations which would have been familiar to the Duke of Wellington. I didn't think the Nazi blitzkrieg on Poland had been achieved that way. However, drill had the intended psychological effect: replacing the individuality of civvy street with the unity of the regiment.

On 9 May 1940, less than a month into our training, the unreality of the Phoney War was shattered when Hitler attacked Denmark, Norway, the Low Countries and France. Our weapons training took on a sense of urgency and purpose. A soldier's best friend is his service rifle and we were drilled thoroughly in its proper care, use and purpose. Ours were Lee Enfield bolt-action rifles, single shot with five-round ammo clips (later ten). We were also introduced to the Bren gun, a Czech-designed light machine-gun with a 30-round magazine. These were the standard British infantry small arms of the day, along with the .38-inch calibre Webley service revolver for officers. I was astonished by the kick from the recoil of the rifle if it was inexpertly held, but once you got the hang of its smooth and fast bolt action the Lee Enfield was a joy to handle. An instructor told us how British troops armed with it halted mass German attacks at Mons in 1914 with fire so rapid that the Germans thought they were facing machine-gunners. It was reliable and accurate up to half a mile, twice that if fired by a marksman. The Bren gun could be fired from the hip but the prone position, with the gunner's mate lying alongside to change magazines, was preferred. It fired up to 450 rounds per minute and often seized up when it got hot. We were taught to loose off effective short bursts rather than just blaze away and to change mags quickly and clear the mechanism when it jammed. I think I could still strip and reassemble a Bren today.

Then there was bayonet training. Shooting practice was obviously necessary but I thought bayonet drill was daft. Despite frontline service throughout the war I never saw a single soldier use his bayonet to deadly purpose, although I dare say some did. We had the usual barrage of commands: 'Squad attenshun. Fix bayonets. Slope arms. Quick march. Charge!' We were shown the straight jab to the belly and the rifle-butt stroke to the face. We practised them repeatedly in lieu of much target practice because there was a shortage of .303 ammo. But I think the army's real interest in cold steel was its ritual, intended to get the adrenaline flowing, stir the blood and arouse the killer instinct. This was stimulated by shouts and curses from our instructors as we charged and lunged at canvas and straw dummies, maniacally roaring our heads off all the while. Bayonet exercises were an excuse to let off steam. We imagined the dummies were the instructors and dealt with them with relish.

They were a mixed bunch. In Balaclava Squad we had one corporal instructor, an old China and North-west Frontier hand, who was foulmouthed and brutal. Others fell in our esteem when we saw the cringing deference they showed towards the officers. Most were good types: older regular army men who behaved according to a code of conduct learned from years of service. Their immaculate turnout, brisk commands and air of authority impressed us all. Off duty they were often approachable, even sensitive, and helped us with problems and grievances. They taught us tricks of the trade: how to keep out of trouble and flannel a way out if landed in it; how to beat the system without overstepping the mark; how to shortcut army bullshit and military bureaucracy that plodded on at peacetime pace. We learned how to look after ourselves and each other, having discovered qualities of tolerance, decency and kindness we shared, especially with those whose backgrounds had done little to foster such character traits. If the army's intention was to dehumanise and brutalise us to fight the Nazis, it was unsuccessful. We were freethinking, egalitarian men at arms, members of a citizen army, not professional killers. Whatever our social conditions had been, six months of the Infantry Training Centre's physical exercise, outdoor life, regular meals and discipline changed us all: we became uniformly smart, fit, confident and proud to be Argylls.

Because I'd been a clerk and could read and write, I was sent to Dundonald camp at Troon to help with the documentation of a new intake of conscripts. I was promoted lance corporal (acting unpaid) and given my first stripe. At the camp I sat at a trestle table, pen in hand and papers in front of me, my stripe lending me brief authority. I felt superior to the nervous, suitcase-carrying civilians who shuffled forth. I'd forgotten that I had been in the same position myself a few months before. I must have had a sneaking sense of the dangerous, corrupting influence of power and the importance and significance of rank in the army, and began to understand better the attitude of the few officers I had been in contact with. I strutted around Glasgow on a visit home welcoming the approach of any passing officers on whom I could practise my well learned salute: 'Longest way up, shortest way down'. I was brought down to earth by my fellow squaddies back at barracks: 'Chancer, scrounger, sergeant's pet', they joked with underlying mockery.

I blotted my copybook only once during initial training. Weekend passes were issued infrequently. I had one and was hurrying down from the Top Square. On the Bottom Square, which I had to cross, a squad had formed for a guard-mounting parade. Unseen by me, around a corner of the Great Hall, stood the duty officer and his sergeant about to march forward to inspect the guard. Impatient to be off I stepped out across the square, arms swinging and giving the officer, when I saw him, my best salute. I was stopped by a furious roar from the sergeant: 'You there. That man. Where the bloody hell d'you think you're going?' I was still ignorant of military etiquette and had interrupted a hallowed ritual. I was made to stand there, mortified and resentful, until the whole thing was over. The officer was too aloof to speak to me, but by Jove the sergeant did. I've never had such a telling-off. My pass was cancelled and I was confined to barracks, where I had time to reflect on the injustices of life.

That incident made me decide to apply for a commission, as soon as I could win myself into favour again. I must have succeeded because Corporal Stewart, the bullying China and North-west Frontier veteran, surprised me by saying I was 'officer material'. I was summoned to a Selection Board. There were three officers on it, all of First World War vintage: a couple of elderly majors and a colonel wearing the red tabs of a staff officer. All three had my papers in front of them and pens at the ready.

The colonel invited me to sit, which I did as if I'd been bolted to the chair. He asked why I wanted to become an officer. I said I needed a challenge, something to aim for. They seemed satisfied by that clichéd response. What I really wanted to say was that I liked the uniform and dreamed of martial glory; that now I was in the army I wanted to get on and make the most of it; that I was attracted by the privileges of rank, its better living conditions and pay; that I was fed up being bossed about by NCOs and that I looked forward to doing some bossing about myself; that I would make as good an officer as some I had met. There were the usual questions about family background, schooling (Hyndland Secondary, which I doubt had any significance for them), civilian occupation, sporting activities and hobbies. It must have been on my record that I was a singer, in church choirs and the Glasgow Orpheus Club, and that I had sung in fund-raising concerts for Forces Charities, because I was asked about that as well. Without stretching the truth too far I presented myself in as good a light as possible. I felt I was playing a game where they had made the rules; felt justified in bending them to my advantage.

I told them my father had been a naval officer, hoping they'd think he'd been a destroyer captain, not merely bandmaster on a pensioned-off sailing ship where orphans and the miscreant youth of Glasgow were given a second chance as cadets. I told them, with some truth, that my favourite writers were Buchan and Kipling. That went down very well. On the strength of frequent swimming sessions at Whiteinch Baths, rambles on the Campsie Fells as a boy and youth hostelling in the Trossachs, where I'd once climbed Ben Venue, I made myself out to be a champion swimmer and skilled mountaineer. When I mentioned cricket, the colonel's eyes lit up.

'Cricket, eh!' he barked. 'Who did you play for?'

I'd anticipated that one. My local Baldwin Cricket Club in the Glasgow Parks League would have meant nothing to him.

'West of Scotland, sir.'

I didn't blink, or mention that I'd only played at their ground and against their second eleven.

'Batsman, eh?' the colonel went on.

'No, sir. Fast bowler.'

I couldn't have done better. The three officers exchanged knowing smiles and made marks with their pens. I was obviously the spirited, fiery aggressive type they wanted. I could tell I had made it when the colonel smiled and said, 'Good man.'

At the end of August 1940 I was posted to 165 Officer Cadet Training Unit (OCTU) at Dunbar, the North Sea fishing and holiday town in East Lothian. Like Stirling it has historic military connections, having been garrisoned during the Napoleonic Wars with troops and artillery on the cliffs near the ruined medieval castle above the harbour. Local militia were based at Castle Park where Lauderdale House, a Georgian mansion, still stands. In 1940 Lauderdale House and the adjacent barracks were the HQ of 165 OCTU and we paraded regularly on Barrack Square, originally the mansion's cliff-top garden. Many cadets from numerous regiments were being trained at Dunbar. Those who passed the course would be commissioned as second lieutenants, posted to a battalion and given the most junior command, a platoon.

The OCTU was organised like a battalion, with four companies, A, B, C and D. Mine was A Company, the recruits' company (the other companies' cadets were already serving soldiers). Every hotel and boarding house in the town had been requisitioned by the War Office to accommodate the training unit's staff, cadets and other military personnel based in the area. My billet was the Roxburghe Marine Hotel where about 100 cadets were quartered, mostly four to a room. I shared digs with two Scots and a Welshman. The hotel, which had a panoramic seaside setting, had been built for Edwardian holiday-makers who once relaxed in its saltwater therapeutic baths. Little remained of that period or its style. The interior, stripped of its furnishings, was reduced to wartime austerity.

Days began with Reveille at 0600 followed by PT. We were used to that but not to swimming exercises at that hour in Dunbar's unheated saltwater pool. After breakfast we were drilled by a formidable team of Scots Guards sergeants armed with pace sticks, powerful voices and a rich vocabulary. They treated us as raw recruits although we'd been through several months of infantry training, and we were not spared the fastidious formalities of kit and room inspections. Afternoons were spent on exercises: constructing fieldworks with entrenching tools and rolls of barbed wire, weapons and vehicle training, artillery observation and signals, map and compass reading; how to note the military significance of topography in sketches and appreciations, handle sections and platoons, and care for men and equipment. In the evenings we studied training manuals and technical papers or attended lectures on the hundred and one other skills an infantry subaltern needed to know. Lights Out was at 2215.

We were required to study the officers' and sergeants' bible, the *Field Service Pocket Book*, a sort of boy scout guide for the infantry. It began with a glossary of military terms and organisation in the field followed with the instruction that it not to be taken into frontline trenches, where it would have been most useful. Among its tips were: what to do with prisoners and captured documents; how to lead a patrol and what to look out for; how to interpret aerial reconnaissance photographs, camouflage your position, block roads with felled trees, defend a building, lay demolition charges; how to purify water, cook with mess tins and camp kettles (recipes for stews included) and camp in 'uncivilised countries'.

We learned the army's operational structure. Section: ten men; three sections, a platoon; three platoons, a company; four companies (plus an HQ company), a battalion; three battalions, a brigade; three brigades, a division; three divisions, a corps; three corps, an army. Infantry companies (nine officers, 120 other ranks) were named A, B, C and D. In the field, three would be active and one in reserve with the HQ company. Each company had machine-gun, mortar, anti-tank and Bren gun carrier platoons or sections, plus two supporting echelons (A and B) to handle logistics. Artillery and armoured support was from attached units.

There was a mantra to memorise: Information (intelligence); Intention (objectives); Method (deployment and weapons); Administration (logistics); Intercommunication (of the preceding points across all levels of command). This formula was, as I found on active service, followed scrupulously at every operational briefing, everything done by the book. Every command was passed down the line, written or spoken (sometimes by radio), in an unambiguous manner and acknowledged. If the command was face to face there would invariably be a final, 'Any questions?' Those were rare: ours was not to reason why.

Our instructors called us 'sir', as in 'Hold that rifle properly, sir.' The courtesy was often tinged with sarcasm when they supervised assault and obstacle courses to measure our courage, route marches our stamina, target practice our marksmanship and written tests our intelligence. We were trained to give orders and to obey them. Among the high standards expected of us were those of 'gentlemen'. The British army in 1940 was stratified according to class. While lords and lairds could no longer raise and command their own regiments, or would-be officers from the landed gentry buy commissions, most army officers still came from privileged social backgrounds, often aristocratic. Many had been to university. Ordinary soldiers rarely rose higher than NCO or warrant officer and few sought, or were encouraged to seek, further promotion. In 1939 the War Office decreed that all recruits whatever their social status had to start in the ranks, but the way candidates were selected for officer training maintained a public school and, as I had found to my advantage, sporting bias. The sons of army brass and landed gentry set the tone in the officers' mess of Scottish regiments, as they had done before the war.

The atmosphere at the OCTU was as I imagined boarding school to be, an impression heightened by Lauderdale House's Georgian architecture. At weekends we were allowed to stay out until midnight. There were Friday night dances at North Berwick Pavilion. Local folk invited us to their homes, clubs and churches. Although the hospitality was generous, we cadets were keen to get on with our training, secure postings to the regiments of our choice and play our part in the war.

The evacuation of Dunkirk had been accomplished against all odds and now the nation faced the threat of a German invasion. The coast was a restricted area. Beaches were fortified with concrete tank traps, artillery, searchlights and ack-ack batteries. Navy ships patrolled the Firth of Forth, whose north shore was defended by Polish troops who had escaped from the Continent. Trenches were dug and landmines planted on the

East Links next to our hotel. Road blocks were manned by enthusiastic but ill-equipped Home Guard volunteers. The Royal Observer Corps had observation posts along the coast, including one at Dunbar. RAF Spitfires swept the skies above a landscape which was ablaze with crops ripening in the glorious weather of that fateful summer of 1940.

On Saturday 7 September we got our first taste of action when the 'Cromwell' balloon went up. Cromwell was the government's code word for an imminent invasion alert. At 2215 hours notices were projected onto the screens of the cinemas calling soldiers and cadets back to their billets; duty officers and military police had to round up those in pubs and other places. Amid excited talk of 'invasion' and the 'real thing' we were organised hastily, issued with basic equipment and five rounds of .303 ammo, and marched off to take up our position on the coast. I was a bit late and fortunately so, as I got a lift in a truck. We knew it wasn't a practice alarm. My platoon spent a miserable night in foxholes in the dunes above Tyninghame sands peering through the gloom towards the sea. For the first few hours we were expecting any moment to see the sea black with ships and the sky black with planes. Nothing happened. We spent the night in a curious state of semi-conciousness, alternately cursing and laughing, and shivering all the time. A state of absolute misery was reached when our cigarettes and chocolate ran out. I was never so pleased to see the sun rise.

Such was our part in that great turning point of the war, the Battle of Britain then being fought in the skies above southern England. As we learned later, invasion might indeed have come had Hitler so ordered. But even in the dark days of defeat in Norway, evacuation of Dunkirk, and disaster in the Far East in 1942, there was never any doubt in the minds of most servicemen and civilians alike that we would eventually emerge victorious in the war. Churchill's rhetoric and leadership were an inspiration to the whole country—as was his dogged defiance of the enemy in his memorable phrase 'Never, never give in' which sustained his fellow countrymen and women, and was cherished as a watchword by many of my generation throughout the rest of our lives.

We were kept at readiness for a week after the Cromwell scare, manning checkpoints and patrolling the coast and countryside. We had a further experience of what real soldiering might be like towards the end of our course. We undertook a three-day, 60-mile training exercise over the Lammermuir Hills. This involved sleeping rough, forced marches over difficult ground and simulated attacks on dummy enemy positions. Our instructors were waiting at the battle-training area. Officers with maps and clipboards sat in open-top staff cars. The assaults were made more realistic by harmless but frightening explosive charges and the occasional burst of live rifle and machine-gun fire over our heads. For two nights we kipped down in the heather under a starry sky. On the third day we followed Whiteadder Water, sleeping in a barn en route to the sea. On the coast road back to Dunbar we stepped and sang 'Pack up your troubles' and popular songs of the time, with ribald variations, a display of careless abandon and high spirits that we were seldom to feel again. We entered Dunbar at sunset, heads held high and rifles at the slope, feeling we could take on the whole German army.

That toughening-up exercise was the final stage of the course which would end with our being judged fit to hold His Majesty's commission, or not; those who failed were returned to the ranks. Those who passed had to be outfitted as second lieutenants in regimental colours for the Passing Out Parade, which required for me a visit to Anderson's Regimental and Highland Tailors on George Street in Edinburgh. The parade was held on Barrack Square. We slow-marched to a haunting pipe tune then took 'Cock o' the North' and 'Hieland Laddie' in quick time. There were drinks in a bar, a round of farewells and home on brief leave before reporting to our various regimental depots. I had arrived at OCTU as a cadet with a white-banded forage cap and left as a second lieutenant in the Argylls with the glengarry I had dreamed of wearing.

At Queen Street train station in Glasgow I could barely find my way. There was fog and I had forgotten about the blackout. I stumbled onto George Square where my old office building, the Cenotaph and statuary loomed out of the gloom. Tramcars squeaked and rumbled, trolley poles sparking. Because Glasgow's shipyards, docks and industries offered plentiful targets for the Luftwaffe many buildings were sandbagged, and windows cross-taped to minimise flying glass from bomb blasts. My parents had an Anderson shelter in the garden in Knightswood, a council estate to which we had moved from the flat in Partick where I was born. I cut quite a dash in my new uniform when I turned up out of the fog. I caught up on family and local news and visited a friend, Chris Mackay. Her dad, Archibald Mackay, my future father-in-law, was in the Home Guard and had served with the Argylls in the First World War.

En route back to Stirling, I had a rendezvous at Buchanan Street station with five fellow subalterns: Ken 'Tattie' Shaw, a former law student from Lancashire I'd met at Dunbar; Gilbert MacDougall, a medical student at Glasgow University who'd given up his studies to volunteer for the Argylls, returning from Bulford OCTU, Wiltshire; Alex 'Sandy' Graham, also a Bulford graduate, formerly a student at the Glasgow School of Art; and two other newly commissioned second lieutenants, MacDonald and McGill. At Stirling we bundled ourselves and our kit into two taxis. We drove up the hill, past the Parade Ground where I had square bashed not so long before, through the arch of the Gatehouse and past other familiar castle landmarks, to draw up at the foot of the steps of the Officers' Mess in the Top Square. There we gathered our kit and ourselves and stood about nervously, unsure what to do or where to go and arguing about who should lead the way. So much for our training in quick thinking, taking command and using our initiative.

Eventually we sorted ourselves out and reported to the Commanding Officer, a kindly First World War veteran who directed us through formalities and showed us to our quarters. I shared a room with Sandy Graham, a bit of a rebel and a humorist, not all that interested in being a soldier (we lost touch during the war, after which he developed his comic and artistic talents and became a well known cartoonist). He and I enjoyed for the first time the privilege of being wakened at Reveille by a batman, bringing us our 'gunfire' mugs of hot sweet tea. In the Officers' Mess we were at the bottom of a rigid pecking order, so it was a relief to be treated with hospitality typical of a Highland regiment. Dinner at our inaugural Mess Night was accompanied by ritual and etiquette: the formal dress, the regimental silver, passing the port around the polished mahogany table and toasts to battle honours. This was our first experience of the luxury of rank and I liked it. Sitting beneath the regimental colours and flags of the past which swayed in and out of focus before my eyes, I felt had joined an élite whose valorous tradition I was destined to uphold.

A few days later the Pipe Major, a man of special standing, initiated us into an unexpected tradition, of early morning lessons in Highland dancing. We didn't take them too seriously until he told us about the winter Regimental Ball and the bonnie lassies from Stirlingshire's aristocracy who would be itching to dance with handsome and accomplished young officers. We found ourselves being saluted by our former NCO instructors and warrant officers. That punctiliousness didn't last. They knew that the makings of a good officer meant more than a fancy uniform, a pip on the shoulder and a swagger stick. They told us so and put us in our places. Second lieutenants were two a penny, now that OCTUs were churning out junior officers by the hundreds for the expanding army.

Nobody bothered us much because we were transients waiting postings. Those of our superiors who did take an interest kept us occupied in routine tasks which we found tedious, impatient as we were to get on with the war. This we knew nothing about, but what it could do to a man was evident in the odd and disturbing behaviour of one officer. He was a survivor of Dunkirk, thought to be 'off his chump'. We wondered what terrifying experiences he'd had that made him cry out at night. By day he would talk and shout commands to his dog, which had been left in France. Later in the war I understood his malaise—once I'd seen more cases of battle fatigue, its causes and felt it myself.

2 Cairo

I was posted to 1st Battalion in the Middle East in December 1940 with Shaw, MacDougall, MacDonald and McGill. I would have preferred 2nd Battalion, the 93rd of Balaclava, then in the Far East. I was later to be grateful for the mysterious workings of Providence that sent me to Egypt instead of Malaya.

I was one of four brothers in the Forces during the war: Cecil joined the Marines, was commissioned and went out to the Far East with 42 Royal Marine Commando; Harold was called up and found himself in the Royal Air Force meteorological branch, in North-west Europe after D-Day; Alex, the eldest, who worked in the Savings Bank, was in the Royal Navy on the aircraft carrier HMS *Implacable* with the Pacific fleet towards the end of the war (the authorities, showing unusual good sense, put him in the paymaster's office). Being the youngest, I was the first to be called up and the first to be posted overseas. Only a few days' embarkation leave were allowed and my memory of them is of awkward farewells. My departure meant the prospect of a long separation—1st Battalion might be deployed anywhere. Soldiers' families faced months or years of anxiety before prayed-for good news and safe returns. All feared the War Office telegram with its blunt summary of wounds or worse. It was a cold morning when I left. I served for six years in the Argylls, most of them overseas with A Company, first as a platoon commander, then second-in-command and finally company commander. I never saw my father again.

We had orders to report to Worcester army depot, to join a draft of men of the Worcester Regiment and accompany them to the Middle East where they were to reinforce their 1st Battalion. We met at Glasgow Central station's rendezvous, a First World War howitzer shell used as a charity box. Groups of soldiers and sailors stood around, some with sweethearts saying goodbye. Our train was packed. We flaunted our travel warrants and rank to secure a compartment and settled down as the train steamed and rumbled across the Clyde. We chatted for a while, joking about the regimental ball we would miss.

At Worcester the five of us, together with two Worcester subalterns, were billeted at Priors Court, a Tudor manor house outside the town. Most days we reported to the depot where we got to know the men of the draft, supervised kit issues and attended parades and inspections. Soldiers in uniform were a familiar sight at that time but our arrival caused something of a stir locally. Few in that part of the country had ever seen a Highland soldier in his eye-catching uniform. For Tattie Shaw, who came from Oldham, and me, English on my mother's side, being south of the border was no novelty but for the three Macs it was foreign territory. They, especially MacDougall, a dour, thrawn fellow of West Highland stock, did not relish the prospect, as proud Argylls, of being associated with men of a mere English county regiment. We were not to know that the Worcesters were to play as heroic a part as any other infantry regiment in the battles that took place later in the Western Desert.

Worcester was Elgar country which I would otherwise have enjoyed, but we had little time for sightseeing or fraternising with the locals. A dance, film show or a fleeting friendship with any girl we were lucky enough to meet were about as far as our socialising went. We were invited for sherry at the house of a retired brigadier who was courteous and cultivated, if a bit of a Colonel Blimp. He had served in the Middle East and insisted on telling us about it. When politeness permitted, we rose to take our leave. 'Silly old bugger,' MacDougall muttered rather uncharitably as soon as were out of earshot.

That winter of 1940–1941 was the coldest in years with frost and snow all around. Priors Court, its eaves festooned with icicles, the interior furnished from army stores, was a bleak billet mercifully kept warm by log fires. There we lived a spartan existence for a few weeks over Christmas and Hogmanay before receiving our marching orders which arrived by dispatch rider:

SECRET: troop convoy No. WS5B, Liverpool.

We entrained for Liverpool with the Worcester draft. At Pier Head station I was shocked to see the damage that aerial bombardment could do in a built-up area. Two air raids just before Christmas had caused widespread destruction, but the port was operating and six liners were waiting to take troops aboard. Ours was HMT (formerly RMS) *Windsor Castle*, one of the finest ships of the Union Castle Line. It had been built in 1921 by John Brown, Clydebank, and modernised in 1937. Now it was a grey-painted troopship, having been requisitioned by the Admiralty at the start of the war. Its hull, patterned with portholes and riveted steel plates, towered above us like a cliff as we clutched our kit and clambered up the gangplank. It took a day for some 2,500 officers and men from various regiments and other units to embark and for their equipment and stores to be loaded on a ship that normally took 600 passengers.

We sailed on the afternoon of 7 January 1941, the *Windsor Castle*'s hooter booming and echoing off the façades of Liverpool's grandiose waterfront buildings. Hundreds of soldiers crowded the decks, leaning on the ship's rails, watching the shore as the light faded. We followed the convoy commodore's flagship, *Athlone Castle*, with the Canadian Pacific liner *Empress of Australia* directly astern of us. Both were transporting Australian and New Zealand troops who had been training in southern England. There must have been some delay in assembling the convoy because we anchored off North Wales. On the evening of the 10th we sailed to Belfast Lough to await ships from the Bristol Channel and the Clyde. At 0500 on Sunday 12 January 1941 our armada of shadowy shapes slipped seaward towards the North Channel where eleven liners from the Clyde joined the convoy. Our last sight of land was of the south coast of Islay. That was a special moment for MacDougall whose people came from Port Charlotte. We had no idea how long we would be at sea. All certainty seemed to vanish in the cold dawn haar.

There were 21 passenger ships. Judging by the number of men on the *Windsor Castle*, there must have been over 40,000 troops in that convoy. There was a powerful escort. The unmistakable silhouette of a battleship squatted on the horizon, along with three cruisers and 12 destroyers. The commodore manoeuvred the troopships into seven columns spread across three miles of ocean, each column with three ships in line ahead, all led by the cruiser *Australia*. Astern were two other cruisers and our battleship, HMS *Ramillies*. The destroyers formed an anti-submarine screen on both beams. Bristling with guns, they sped about churning up white bow waves. One of the cruisers surged past, raising its big guns skywards, and loosed off a volley from its pom-poms in practice ack-ack fire. Signallers flashed Morse code messages from Aldis lamps. We had an air escort for a while. Then the convoy began to zig-zag, an anti-submarine measure.

We exceeded the ship's peacetime complement by a factor of four and I doubted that there were enough lifeboats. We didn't complain when we were obliged to take turns on anti-submarine watch. Twice a day, sirens sounded 'Boat Stations' for abandon ship drill. At night, a blackout was enforced. I had never been so far out to sea and the experience was exciting and unnerving. At the purser's office a map of the ship's prewar route from Southampton to Cape Town and Durban was still pinned up, along with notices for deck games, dances and shore excursions to Madeira. We never saw Madeira. To avoid U-boats we sailed in the pale winter sun on a semicircular cruise that seemed to be taking us first to Canada. The weather was freezing. Battledress and greatcoats barely kept us warm. 'Look out for icebergs,' Mac said. No one laughed. The destroyers, searching for U-boats, danced around in a fascinating daily choreography.

At least we travelled in style, the officers that is. The first-class dining room and other upper deck facilities on board the *Windsor Castle* were still organised on a peacetime basis. We enjoyed four- or five-course meals served by Union Castle Line stewards, and comfortable two- and four-berth Cabines-de-Luxe. The ship was less of a holiday for the other ranks, living and messing together as they were compelled to do in cramped quarters below decks. The injustice revealed by this contrast between the lifestyles of officers and men almost made me turn socialist. Experiences such as these no doubt influenced thousands of servicemen in casting their votes in the postwar General Election, which was a Labour landslide victory.

The weather warmed up after the convoy turned south. We began to feel we were out of danger, having seen neither U-boats nor encountered winter storms. The ship's officers appeared in gleaming white tropical kit and scanned the horizon with their binoculars. We discarded our winter gear for khaki shorts, shirts and solar topees. On 25 January we sighted a peninsula of mangroves, palm trees and vivid green hills. This was Freetown, Sierra Leone, one of the few ports of call on the convoy routes to and from the Indian Ocean. There we had our first glimpse of the mysterious mountains of the Dark Continent. My knowledge of Africa had come from reading the novels of Conrad, Buchan and Rider Haggard. That knowledge was soon to be considerably enlarged.

Freetown's anchorage was crowded. The *Windsor Castle* slowed as if smitten by the heat and anchored inside an anti-submarine boom. Flotillas of filthy bumboats and oil barges came alongside. Army and air force chaps en route came aboard with news and gossip. Others were ferried ashore, where tin roofs and wood and brick colonial buildings receded to a range of hills coated with steaming rainforest. We were not allowed shore leave at that malarial, malodorous anchorage, where our only amusement was the antics of natives who paddled out in long, slim dugout canoes which bobbed in the swell. Trading with Africans was against army regulations but we lowered rope baskets with tins of bully beef and army blankets, and hauled up melons and bunches of bananas. The younger natives dived for coins we threw. Their grinning black faces would surface with sixpenny pieces sparkling between gleaming white teeth, to be greeted with laughter and howls of racist abuse from the squaddies.

After four days in Freetown's fetid bay the ship's crew turned saltwater hoses on the canoes to drive them away as we raised anchor. The convoy re-formed and we settled into our closed world. We sat on deck sunbathing and reading or played deck games. Among the duties of subalterns accompanying drafts of reinforcements was to keep the troops fit with PT and marches on the promenade decks, and alert by giving occasional talks. Since none of us had any experience of warfare our pro-

31

nouncements must have seemed far from convincing. An entertainment committee organised plays and concerts. We had a boisterous Crossing the Line ceremony. Now that we were in the tropics, the men were allowed to sleep in the fresh air out on deck. At night, the sky was lit by myriads of unfamiliar stars; by day it billowed with distant cumulus clouds. I marvelled at the southern sea's phosphorescence and dolphins and flying fish darting in and out of the water; at the seemingly limitless expanse on which we sailed and the ocean covering the wake of our great liner as if it had never been there.

After a month at sea we awoke one morning to find that half the convoy had veered off to Cape Town during the night. Three days later we approached Durban and saw the city gleaming in the sunlight. The people of Natal were patriotic. Durban city centre was solidly British colonial with institutions, architecture and names to match. We received enthusiastic cheers from a crowd on the quay, and families came to the docks to invite us to their homes for lunch or tea. We were welcomed everywhere we went. Every troopship that docked at Durban received the same attention.

Shaw had found a Union Castle brochure advertising safaris to big-game reserves. The closest we came to the bushveld were the animal trophies on the wall and skin rugs on the wooden floors of a country club where we were invited to lunch. We enjoyed excellent food and wine served by impassive black servants in an atmosphere Kipling and Rider Haggard would have felt at home in. They would have felt saddened, as we were, to see Zulus, members of a noble warrior race, plying a humble trade as rickshaw men in the city. I didn't care much for the smug bearers of the White Man's burden at the country club. Our small talk was confined to safe territory: the empire, cricket and the war. I don't know if the word 'apartheid' was used then but its existence was apparent everywhere. Many Afrikaners were pro-German, yet South Africans were serving with General Wavell's army in the Western Desert.

We changed ship at Durban. The Cape Town ships rejoined us at sea. Four liners, including the *Windsor Castle*, steamed away for Bombay.

After another week or so, we passed the Horn of Africa, saw the mountains of Arabia and steamed into the Red Sea. Suez was felt before we saw it. A wave of heat enveloped the ship. To port and starboard, red hills shimmered in the haze. A mirage, a phenomenon I would soon get used to, drifted along the coast. Strange shapes materialised as mosques, oil tanks and barrage balloons, and smudges on the water solidified into a score of ships at anchor. We disembarked at Port Tewfiq, a man-made spit of land at the southern entrance to the Suez Canal. It had been built with fill from the canal diggings and it was where we were unceremoniously dumped into the sights, sounds and smells of Egypt. We boarded a train which steamed off slowly. A sea of eager eyes, white teeth and black and brown faces washed up against it. We were besieged by beggars; hawkers tried to jump aboard, screaming at us to buy their cheap cigarettes, soft drinks and dirty postcards. Such was our baffling landfall on 8 March 1941. We had been at sea for two months and sailed 15,000 miles.

The train steamed north along a dreary desert corridor. The canal, on a parallel course on our right, drifted in and out of view making the funnels and upper decks of ships appear like wrecks marooned in the sands. Those of us who had imagined an ancient land of palm-fringed oases were disappointed as we passed army camps and ack-ack guns, and mud-brick villages barely distinguishable from the desert. There was no relief from the stink of coal smoke, from the hard wooden seats, the heat, and the hawkers at every stop. That inauspicious first impression coloured our subsequent dealings with the Egyptians, few of whom we trusted and most of whom, I suspect, despised us in return. They had no love for the British empire, having long been part of the Ottoman one. In the 1860s, while the Suez Canal was being dug, Egypt's French-educated ruler, Khedive Ismail, began to modernise the country and bankrupted the state. The British invaded in 1882, primarily to secure the canal. When the First World War began, the government in London declared Egypt a protectorate. Those events and the recent influx of soldiers from Britain and the empire, to counter the threat of invasion by Mussolini's army in North

Africa, did not affect Egypt's essential character: its antiquity, Islamic courtesies, heat, dust and squalor.

I remember the desert air turning cold after dusk when we arrived at the township of Geneifa, south of Ismailiya, 100 kilometres east of Cairo. We tumbled off the train and marched to the Infantry Base Depot where we were relieved of our responsibility for the Worcesters, who were to join their battalion then in Eritrea. In the dark the depot looked like a set from one of those postwar PoW escape films. The next day we found that we were living like ants in a small part of a vast camp whose orderly rows of tents and wooden huts stretched away into the desert. This was where soldiers new to Egypt were sent for acclimatisation, desert training and postings to their regiments. There were hundreds of men of all types and nationalities: Australians, New Zealanders, South Africans, Indians and British, a cross section of Wavell's desert army which had just routed Mussolini's forces, before the German Afrika Korps entered the fray. Most were drafts of reinforcements but we also saw suntanned and sharp- or glazed-eyed desert hands hurrying purposefully to and fro in transit, returning from courses, or recovering from sickness, battle fatigue or wounds. We regarded these veterans with awe. They returned our interest with a mixture of sympathy and superiority, and called us 'pinkies' until we acquired their desert tans. Anyone with a few weeks in Egypt proclaimed expert status. Some officers had evidently wangled cushy jobs at the depot. Far from being old desert hands, they had no intention of straying further than the services' clubs and fleshpots of Cairo.

We trotted or staggered to and from the latrines during the first few weeks. Few newcomers to Egypt were exempt from gyppo tummy, or prickly heat, dysentery and typhus, or lice picked up from infected blankets. A regular stream of orders and instructions descended on unit commanders stressing the need for cleanliness and sanitation. But human nature being what it is they were not always followed strictly, especially among large bodies of troops where the risk of infection was highest. Even those most dedicated to the cause of health and hygiene fought a losing battle against the constant menace of flies, bugs and parasites.

Occasionally we escaped from the camp to the Bitter Lakes where we swam in clear and buoyant water. Within weeks I was as bronzed as any desert warrior. Some evenings we were entertained under the stars at the camp's outdoor cinema (bench seats for the men and wicker chairs for officers) where, through a haze of dust, cigarette smoke, flying bugs and moths, films were projected onto a canvas screen.

It was after one of those shows that one of our gang got himself arrested. He had been a friend of MacDougall's at university and was now a second lieutenant in the Highland Light Infantry. To relieve the monotony of our existence we would go into Ismailiya for a drink and a meal at the Officers' Club and wander round the town. One evening this bold lad, having had too much to drink and fancying perhaps that he was in the wild west town in the film we'd just seen, went on the rampage. Recklessly he started to take pot shots at street lamps with his revolver. The few Egyptians who were about fled for cover as we tried to restrain him, to no avail. Soon the sheriff arrived in the shape of a lieutenant and two other members of the Military Police. The luckless subaltern was disarmed and placed under close arrest. A court martial followed and he was cashiered and sent back to the UK. It was to his credit that he overcame that disastrous setback to his military career and made good by regaining his commission and serving in another regiment.

Word of the 'shoot-out at the Bitter Lake' got around, so we were lucky to be allowed day passes to Cairo. Most of the way the road ran alongside the Sweetwater Canal, a misnamed ditch linking the Suez Canal with the Nile. At the drop-off point at Ramses railway station hordes of hawkers and crippled, diseased beggars even more numerous than those at Port Tewfiq held forth hands for baksheesh and yelled abuse when ignored. Every mode of transport invented seemed to be on the streets, from donkeys to big American cars. Pavements were packed with shoeshine boys, street vendors, taxi touts, and groups of off-duty soldiers keeping together. Negotiating these obstacles I felt that MacDougall's contempt for the local riff-raff, 'bloody wogs' as he put it, was amply justified. If the Italians and Germans had taken Cairo, they too would have been greeted with the hawkers' obsequious truculence and cheated at every transaction.

Cairo was the HQ of Middle East Forces, with General Headquarters in a villa by the Nile, but you wouldn't have known there was a war on. There was no rationing, or shortage of goods in the department stores, and there was no blackout except when air-raid sirens sounded, which they did at times. But the city was not bombed because the Italians hoped the Egyptians would welcome them, and Churchill had let it be known that if Mussolini raided Cairo the RAF would bomb Rome. The press was censored except, it seemed, for society columns and propaganda, the authorities being obsessed with keeping the Egyptians in awe of British power. Soldiers who knew the reality of retreat, after the Afrika Korps arrived in Tripoli in February 1941 to aid the Italians, scoffed at the 'jolly good show' journalese. At Shepheard's Hotel, where the Moorish-style lobby had two Nubian caryatids whose voluptuous breasts were well polished, having been fondled by three generations of British officers, there seemed no enemy threat. British civil servants and base wallahs put in a few hours' work in the mornings and spent afternoons at Shepheard's, or Groppi's Parisian-style café, or the Gezira Club on an island on the Nile. I recall watching a cricket match there, bought books at Librairie La Renaissance d'Egypt and saw *Merrie England* at Cairo Opera House, an Italian-designed building opened in 1869 to celebrate the completion of the Suez Canal. It was ironic that the auditorium on that occasion resounded to the strains of an English operetta, at a time when the Italians were still smarting from their crushing defeat not so far away in the Western Desert.

Another remembered highlight of the unreality of wartime Cairo in 1941 was a visit to the Sphinx and climbing the great Pyramid of Giza, accompanied by an Egyptian guide and a Scots Guards officer I met at the base depot. The sun was dipping into the desert as we pulled ourselves up the monument's stone blocks. From the summit its shadow pointed to Cairo where the domes and minarets of the old city glinted in the haze. I ran my hand over some graffiti. The most eroded marks were French, Napoleon's soldiers now forgotten. Back in the city I took a tour, with an elderly Arab guide, of Old Cairo's souks and mosques. They remained a mystery to most of us as we rarely strayed from the European quarter's French boulevards. The army's guidebook to Cairo listed approved hostels and clubs, like the Services Club at Ezbekieh Gardens which put on dances and concerts to which members of HM Forces were 'invited to bring their lady friends'. The book did not mention the Berka red light district, for many soldiers the city's main attraction.

We had been without mail for over two months while we were at sea and it took some time for it catch up with us—I must say that thereafter the service was efficient, mail being recognised by the army as essential for morale. In this instance it was disturbing, with first-hand accounts of the air raids on two consecutive nights in mid-March when hundreds of German bombers attacked Clydeside. We read about the raids with mixed feelings but mostly those of relief that our families were safe and well. My parents and brothers heard the German bombers overhead and were shaken by one near miss as they huddled inside the Anderson shelter in the garden. It was awful to think of my parents going through those nights of terror while I was enjoying life on the high seas on the *Windsor Castle*. The fact that our families were in danger and as much in the front line as any combatant gave us an added sense of purpose and a better grasp of why we were fighting. We were eager to get on with it and impatient for our postings to come through. When they did they brought disappointment for me.

The Argylls were training at the Combined Operations Centre at Kabrit on the Great Bitter Lake. It seemed that four officers only were required at that time and since their names were picked alphabetically MacDonald, MacDougall, McGill and Shaw were sent off and I was left behind. I felt downcast not only at being parted from my friends and forced to stay at the Base Depot but also at the thought of missing out on whatever action they might see with the battalion before I joined them again. The Germans had invaded Greece. In the Western Desert the Afrika Korps had advanced to the Egyptian frontier and Tobruk was under siege. The battalion was moved to the desert to dig defences and guard airfields. I found myself spending more time in Cairo, on a course at the Middle East Tactical School. I suppose I should have been grateful the luck of the draw served me so well then because in May the battalion was sent from the desert to disaster on Crete. If I had gone with them the odds are that I would not have come back.

The Argylls landed at Tymbaki on the south coast of Crete. They suffered heavy casualties in the confusion after the Germans launched a massive paratroop assault on the island's north coast. Half the battalion remained at Tymbaki to defend the beach and airfields for reinforcements which never came. The CO, Lieutenant-Colonel Anderson, led the other half through the mountains to the north coast to aid the 14th Infantry Brigade at Heraklion. Lieutenant Jock Hamilton of A Company told me how, armed with a rifle and 50 rounds, he had hidden in a ditch and helped break up an enemy dawn attack, shooting Germans until his ammo ran out. When the CO congratulated him Jock had replied, 'The place was hoaching with Jerries. I couldn't miss, sir.' But individual acts of courage on Crete were not enough in the face of overwhelming odds.

One of those killed was Allan MacDonald, one of the of the five young Argyll subalterns who had sailed with the Worcester draft a few months before. He was a West Highlander from Oban of proud and fiery spirit and we, his friends, felt his loss keenly. Of the battalion's men of all ranks 300 were left behind on the south coast and taken prisoner. Those on the north coast were evacuated at night aboard Royal Navy destroyers but had to endure dive bombing by Stukas en route to Alexandria. Out of a battalion 655 strong that had embarked just ten days earlier only 312 returned. That number was later increased when a score of men, after incredible adventures on land and sea, managed to escape and return by devious routes. Nine Jocks posted as 'missing' reappeared after escaping from the south coast of Crete with around 60 other Allied soldiers and nine officers. Their motor launch was stopped by an Italian submarine. The Italians took the officers for questioning but let the men sail on. Navigating with an army compass they reached the North African coast at Mersa Matruh, having sailed 300 miles. Despite the grim statistics of Crete and all that I heard from those who survived the fighting and made a safe return to Egypt, and all that I have read about the campaign since, I have always regretted not taking part. Having known many of those who did I appreciate what it meant to them to be able to say with pride, 'I was in the Battle of Crete.'

Survivors from Crete were sent to Qassasin desert camp, about 20 kilometres west of Ismailiya, where the battalion was reinforced and reorganised. I was one of seven officers and 350 new men who joined it there, before it was moved to Alexandria on 14 June by overnight train. When we arrived in 'Alex' at 0600 we formed up and marched to Mustapha barracks. I was followed to my quarters by one of the new men. He saluted, introduced himself as Private Walter Sanders and reported for duty as my batman. I had forgotten I was due that privilege of rank.

Sanders had been the janitor at the Bible Training Institute in Glasgow where he lived in the attic of its Gothic-style building. He was devout and abstemious. He must have been unique in the Argylls for I never once heard him utter a blasphemous word, or saw him smoke or take a drink. That fastidiousness was enough to set him apart from his fellows, most of whom drank whenever they got the chance, smoked like chimneys and swore like proverbial troopers. He disapproved of my occasional lapses into insobriety but was tolerant otherwise, always reliable and blessed with a pawky sense of humour, like a couthy character from Walter Scott. He always gave me his beer and cigarette rations. 'Waste not, want not, sir', he'd say as he handed them over. That saying might have been engraved on his heart, such was the pride he took in thrift. He was a tiny island of order in the waste and extravagance of the war. He often spoke of himself in the third person. His favourite refrain to me, other than his biblical ones, was, 'I'm thinking it's the lucky man you are with Sanders to take proper care of your kit.' Each day he woke me with a cry, 'Shake a leg, sir!' Then he'd rustle up his trademark breakfast of tea and pancakes. He cheerfully looked after me like a mother hen.

I was given command of the 30 men in 9 Platoon, A Company. Most of them had arrived with the new draft, so I was not the only rookie. Having missed the expedition to Crete I felt out of touch and not entirely confident, but my company commander, Captain Ted Tidmarsh, made me feel part of his team. He was a splendid regular soldier, commissioned from the ranks early in the desert war and a veteran of the pivotal battles on Crete and at Sidi Barrani, where he had been wounded and Mentioned in Dispatches. Some of the hardened regulars were veterans of the Northwest Frontier and Palestine before the war. I was lucky with my platoon sergeant, Alexander Bloomfield, a regular soldier who had joined the army in 1936 as an 18-year-old Territorial. He came from Greenock, the port on the Clyde, and he was better-groomed than any ship's captain. His impeccable dress and manly bearing set a standard that he expected of us all, particularly impetuous junior officers like me. He understood my evident lack of experience and became my constant guide with his advice, efficiency and loyalty. Kipling once wrote: 'The backbone of the army is the non-commissioned man.' Sergeant Bloomfield, until I found my feet, was mine.

We were in Alex for security duties: airfield and harbour defence; guarding PoW pens full of Italians; general policing, especially to control civil disturbances or looting during air raids. Suez and the Canal Zone were raided often but Alexandria took the brunt of the attacks. It was the navy's main base in the eastern Mediterranean and a departure point for Malta convoys and supply runs to Tobruk. The raids while frequent, sometimes nightly, were ineffective. The bombers flew high to avoid ack-ack and rarely pressed home their attacks.

I was getting to know the other officers and the men in A Company when Captain Tidmarsh sent me on a four-week junior officers' course at the Middle East Weapon Training School (MEWTS) in Palestine. I felt that those who had recently been in action deserved a break from battalion duty, but my friends said that they didn't need weapon training after Crete. I left Alex by train for El Qantara where passengers to Palestine crossed the canal to the railhead of the Sinai railway. It had been built across the desert during the First World War to supply Allenby's offensive against the Turks, the campaign made famous by the exploits of Lawrence of Arabia. Since that time British administrators and energetic Zionists had brought progress to Palestine's biblical byways. I found the Arabs courteous, if sullen. Despite having helped defeat the Turks, they had been betrayed by the British and French at Versailles and now felt dispossessed by Jewish immigration. Before the war there had been an Arab revolt, which the Argylls helped suppress by searching villages for guerrilla fighters and weapons. In March 1940 the battalion had to quell Jewish protests in Tel Aviv. Peacekeeping was a role the Jocks neither relished nor had expected when they joined the army.

The MEWTS was at Bir Salem, on a low ridge by the Jaffa to Jerusalem road. The climate was salubrious, as was the location among cypress and eucalyptus groves and orchards. We enjoyed an active, open-air life free from the infections of Egypt. The training area was centred around a commandeered Lutheran mission, the very place where Allenby had set up his HQ after the capture of Jerusalem in 1917. I shared accommodation with British, Australians and New Zealanders in a two-storey stone schoolhouse. We were all greenhorns with no battle experience but used to the PT, drill and bayonet training we got. More stimulating were lectures on tactics, with emphasis on desert fighting and instruction on infantry weapons including the 'tommy gun', the Thomson submachine-gun supplied by the Americans, favoured by Chicago and Hollywood gangsters. It was all very exciting, the perfect summer camp for hot-blooded young men.

We enjoyed an open-air swimming pool and an occasional meal and drink at a nearby officers' club, with the added attraction of nurses from a military hospital not far away. I spent a happy time with one of them and met her again several times in Alex and Cairo. Later she become engaged to a doctor in the Royal Army Medical Corps, so that was the end of our brief romance. I managed to make a few day trips into Jerusalem and visited Bethlehem, where the area round the Church of the Nativity was woefully commercialised. In Jerusalem Allenby and Lawrence had walked through the Jaffa Gate to be greeted by liberated citizens. I was surrounded by gharry drivers and souvenir sellers. Nevertheless, the influence of my devout parents, a church-going background, scripture studies and a love of psalms and hymns made me receptive to the ancient Biblical resonances of those places.

When I got back to Alex at the end of July I found that the officers and men of the battalion had gone. There were no orders or messages. Then I bumped into Shaw. He persuaded me to stay on in Cairo at Qasr al-Nil Barracks, where he was to play a legal part in a court-martial and rejoin the battalion when his duties were over. The court-martial was delayed so we hung about in Alex for some weeks. No duties, time on our hands and money in our pockets. We swam in the sea through rolling breakers, went on the spree and had a high old time. I am ashamed to think now that while battles were raging in the Western Desert we were living the life of Riley; at Stanley Bay, the Union club, Pastroudis Café, and the Cecil Hotel on the Corniche. The bar at the Cecil, a source of much uncensored information, had never been busier. It was a watering hole for desert army officers. It fairly brimmed with them, and a hotchpotch of navy and RAF types, Waafs, Wrens, Free French, Levantine merchants, Balkan riff-raff, war correspondents and spies. The producers of the film *Casablanca* could have taken it as their model.

Our day of reckoning came when we were returned to the Infantry Base Depot at Ismailiya. There we joined a draft of reinforcements fresh from the UK. We had not long to wait before orders came through. We reported to Suez from where we sailed for Massawa in Eritrea. As we steamed out of Port Tewfiq we passed a wrecked troopship half-submerged, beached and rusting after being bombed. We were to see many more wrecked ships shortly.

3 Abyssinia

We sailed on the *Westernland*, a wheezing, geriatric steamer built in 1917 that had been fitted out for the North Atlantic, not the tropics. The azure of the Red Sea and the coral sand on the red desert shores were intense. The heat was breathtaking, even when we stood by the rail to catch the limp breeze the old steamer's progress aroused. Its teak decks were scorching. Metal fittings burned fingers at the touch. Our cabins were oppressive. Prickly heat plagued us. The food, army tinned bully beef, spilled from its containers like steaming farmyard slops. The lavatories stank and so did we as we sweated on the week's voyage to Massawa.

Allied troops had captured the town from the Italians in April. To open its port for navigation, minesweepers swept the narrow approach channels that flowed between barren islands and coral reefs. We had plenty of time to observe these because, instead of docking, the *Westernland* anchored offshore. Only one vessel at a time could enter the harbour and several ships were waiting. So we spent a further miserable night aboard our good ship before being ferried ashore in bumboats in the morning.

We could not have disembarked at a more dismal backwater. The entrance channels and the harbour were blocked by a disabled Italian destroyer and half-submerged merchant ships methodically scuttled at anchor. Other ships were beached or waterlogged by the quays. Cranes had been blown up and had toppled into the harbour and warehouses were wrecked. The town, the gateway to the Italian East African empire, was built on two islands linked by a causeway to the mainland. Before the war it might have been picturesque, almost Venetian. Its most prominent building was a domed and arcaded nineteenth-century palazzo built for the Ottoman governor, from where the Italian commander, Admiral Bonetti, before surrendering, had ordered the port to be destroyed.

This was where the battalion had landed, from the same ship, at the end of July. We hung around the docks panting like dogs, watching salvage crews sweating aboard the wrecked ships. Paint peeled from *Viva Il Duce* slogans on warehouse walls. I wondered how in this climate there could be much enthusiasm for anything. Mussolini had ordered Bonetti to fight to the last man, but the Italians had already been defeated in the interior. Asmara, the colonial capital, capitulated on April Fool's Day, appropriately because plans of Massawa's defences were found there. The British commander's staff invited Bonetti to surrender, by telephone (it was that sort of war) from Asmara, adding that their CO, Lieutenant-General Sir William Platt, would not be responsible for feeding the 50,000 or so Italians in the capital if the port was sabotaged. Bonetti blew it up anyway. He was captured at the palazzo, surveying the wreckage.

A column of 15-cwt trucks turned up and we were relieved to be told we were leaving immediately for Asmara, 100 kilometres away in the airy uplands of the interior. Thus we began a trek that would take us eventually to Gondar in deepest Abyssinia, 400 kilometres as the crow flies. We were not crows. The road was paved and ran across salt flats towards a seemingly impenetrable escarpment which we had seen from the ship the day we arrived. Soon we were swallowed by lightly forested glens. We emerged from these to face an endless succession of steep curves and hairpin bends clinging to fearsome rock- and cacti-strewn screes. A railway built by Italian engineers and Eritrean labour at the turn of the century swept elegantly through tunnels and across stone-built viaducts as it climbed from the coast. Like the road it was a superb piece of engineering and I soon wished I was on it.

The mountainous scenery, when I dared open my eyes to see it, was as melodramatic as any Victorian painting of Glencoe. Each sharp turn offered a new prospect of disaster. Our drivers, mad Indian Army Service Corps men, charged up the tortuous road which in 50 kilometres climbed to 2,000 metres. Unwilling to lose momentum as the trucks laboured on the inclines, the drivers crashed through the gears and took each bend at full speed, hunched at their steering wheels and turning at the last moment to avoid flying into the abyss. There were no safety barriers.

Below my truck's running board all I could see were dizzying drops. My driver was elated when the road levelled out on the Eritrean plateau. I was dazed with relief. Except in dreams later, I never saw that road again.

The air was fresh, under immense cloudless skies. We were surrounded by rocky and terraced hillsides. Faraway peaks floated on the horizon. Because of the recent monsoon we were halted by road crews repairing washed-out culverts. At one such stop, smoking and chatting with Shaw who was riding in another truck, I heard a rumbling to the south that echoed like artillery fire. A furious electrical storm was blasting the peaks, a distant deluge that accentuated the otherworldliness of the landscape and our expedition. The rains had produced a cornucopia of vegetation and bubbling streams. After the steaming purgatory of the coast it seemed we had found a garden of Eden. The Italians had been ruthless in their conquest and exploitation of this part of East Africa but they had evidently brought many benefits: the road and railway, eucalyptus woodland and irrigation for crops and fruit trees. In the countryside they built tidy townships in the image of home for settlers who came out from Italy. They lost it all because of Mussolini's war.

My driver grinned as he pointed to an Italian road sign: 'Asmara, altitudine, m 2,350'. Suddenly, we were on the palm-lined avenues of an elegant colonial town. The battalion was based at Officio Genio barracks where I found my billet and Sanders, who fixed me with a mock-reproachful gaze through his wire-frame spectacles.

'Mug of tea, sir?' he said and then gave me his impish smile.

Bloomfield's greeting was cooler.

'Thought we'd never see you again, sir.'

I sensed some furtive gossip among the men. Bloomfield had seen it all before: the young platoon commander missing the boat. I had to win his confidence because if I didn't he and the men would be reluctant to follow me anywhere. My limited experience in the army told me that their trust and respect were conditional, rank notwithstanding. As I dumped my kit, Sanders told me the battalion had sweltered for four days at Port Sudan while the *Westernland* took on coal, and at Massawa three companies were bundled into diesel railcars while baggage, the CO's staff car and A Company went by the road. 'Some road, sir,' he observed.

Captain Tidmarsh appeared. 'The CO wants to see you. At the double!'

Lieutenant-Colonel Anderson was a legendary figure, easily recognised by his habit of wearing a faded glengarry and white mackintosh. Those who knew him well called him 'Andy'. I never got that far. The rest of us nicknamed him 'Cockle-ankles' because of his hobbling walk, the result of bullet wounds in France where he had been a company commander and won an MC during the First World War. Between the wars he was with 2nd Battalion in China and Hong Kong. He served in Palestine with 1st Battalion and led it at Sidi Barrani and Crete. So it was with some trepidation that I entered his office, stood to attention and saluted him smartly. He had a greying moustache and hair but his face was suntanned and he looked fighting fit. When he rose from behind an antique Italian desk he was obviously ready to give me a good kicking. He demanded an explanation for my late return from the weapons course in Palestine. I put up a spirited defence and made excuses, although I knew I had none.

'Where's your initiative, man?' he countered. 'You could have hitched with the navy or the air force. I've got men here who made it back from Crete quicker than you.' He waved a sheet of paper at me. 'I was about to have you struck off and returned to Ismailiya.'

I was fortunate to escape severe military discipline. My future conduct would be watched. He let me off with an almighty rocket.

'Ward, you're lucky to keep your pip!'

The Argylls had taken over garrison duties from the Highland Light Infantry and the Worcesters in Asmara, where a PoW camp at Fort Baldissera was guarded and administered. The Italian military in East Africa had surrendered in May. But more than 20,000 Italian and native soldiers were holding out in northern Abyssinia at the old imperial capital of Gondar. Their presence tied down British and Commonwealth forces needed for the defence of Egypt. The Argylls had been sent down the Red Sea to help mop them up. We sent out weekly patrols on the road to Gondar but the enemy made no attempt to take the offensive.

Asmara enjoys a glorious climate and we reckoned it was one of the better stations we served in. It had all the trappings of an Italian colony, founded in 1885. The governor lived in a villa set in bougainvillea-draped parkland; the bishop celebrated Mass in a Romanesque-style red-brick cathedral; there was a Piazza Roma complete with a baroque fountain and a Banca d'Italia. There was none of the dilapidation of Massawa or the destitution and beggary of Cairo. Wide tree-lined streets were graced by modern buildings: a Fiat dealership, Neapolitan cafés, a Cinema Imperio (now screening British newsreels). Mussolini had created a showpiece capital of pastel-coloured art deco architecture no more than five years old. Some of it still bore Il Duce's sinister motto: *Credere, Obeddire, Combattere* (Believe, Obey, Conquer).

I was astonished to see Carabinieri on traffic duty and Italian bureaucrats working under British administration. Relations had been good before the war, when the anglophile Duke of Aosta, Viceroy of Abyssinia, was a frequent guest of British governors at Khartoum and Nairobi. When he surrendered, his request for 'honours of war'—conceding defeat without being disarmed first—was granted. His word ensured that the Italian weaponry was handed over without sabotage and he could maintain his dignity and the pretence that the war in East Africa had been a gentlemanly affair. Perhaps it was for him, but during Mussolini's invasion of Abyssinia in 1935 atrocities had been committed by both sides.

We had regular cigarette and beer rations (there was no shortage of the local Melotti beer, the brewery having been kept open as an essential military service). Electricity from the power station at Massawa had been restored and power lines repaired, so we were able to go to the pictures and the occasional dance, where our attempts at fraternisation with Italian girls were thwarted by wary mothers and aunts. MacDougall, Shaw and I drove around on off-duty jaunts with McGill in a brand-new, soft-top Fiat Topolino which he had acquired somehow, until Cockle-ankles put a stop to such flamboyance and commandeered the car for Battalion HQ. Most of all, I remember Asmara's special sound: the muezzin in the mosque and the cathedral's bells at the start of each day. Each week we added the bagpipes to that duet, when our kilted band paraded along Viale Mussolini to impress the locals.

A and C companies left Asmara on 1 November to join the 12th African Division on the road to Gondar. B Company had already gone, having been ordered to Wadi Halfa on the Nile, from where it was flown to the Libyan desert to garrison Kufra oasis, the HQ of the Long Range Desert Group. D Company stayed on at Fort Baldissera. We drove on an asphalt road into Abyssinia where we passed newly built but now deserted settlements. We saw no Italians in the countryside. Guerrilla fighters and bandits roamed the land. In every valley we saw clusters of conical, grass-roofed mud huts from which natives peered, and children shouted and scraggy dogs barked at us. We bivouacked at Adwa where, in 1896, an invading Italian army was scattered by a native attack which killed 6,000 Italians and askaris. The memory of that humiliation provoked Mussolini's brutality when the Italians invaded again in 1935. At Aksum, once the Queen of Sheba's capital, we saw numerous obelisks. One of the largest had been dismantled and shipped to Rome for Mussolini's pleasure. But Il Duce's minions failed to find Aksum's other treasures: it is said by Abyssinian Christians that the Ark of the Covenant lies there and that the mountains hide King Solomon's mines.

The air on that high plateau in East Africa was freezing at night and the sky glittered with stars which enveloped our elevated camps. After Stand-to we would snuggle down in our bivvies and lie there listening to jackals howling. We woke to the hooting, honking and screeching of birds and unseen creatures. We would eat, strike camp, load the trucks and leave as if we had never been there. Far away to the south, through fantastic tangles of vegetation, the Simien mountains appeared in dreamy clarity rising above canyons and islands of tabletop hills to 4,500-metre cloudy peaks. Abyssinian emperors once retreated into this formidable splendour to escape enemies, or lure them to destruction. Bloomfield thought the landscape looked ideal for ambush, like the North-west Frontier. To traverse the Tekeze gorge we negotiated 12 kilometres of hairpin bends. Wolchefit pass, which had been seized from the Italians a month before, was a similarly daunting obstacle. We camped at Dabat, a bleak moorland fuel dump and airstrip 50 kilometres from Gondar. Then the CO recce'd the road ahead and was shot at. We were sent into action.

Our orders were to attack, capture and hold 'Venticinque', a 200-metre-high ridge overlooking the road 25 kilometres from Gondar. It was one of several points the Italians had fortified on the approaches to the town. These features were about to be assaulted by co-ordinated Allied units. We studied sketches and maps, drawn by intelligence officers and the division's Survey Section to plot the enemy positions. We took over from the 3/6th King's African Rifles on the night of 14–15 November, on a ridge identified in army lingo as Green Hill. As we climbed we were passed by a single file of black soldiers descending, all smiles and white teeth gleaming in the dark as they whispered greetings of 'Jambo, bwana'. At dawn as the mist rose we saw Venticinque across a savannah-like valley, a kilometre or so west of our position. Beyond it lay Ambazzo Hill, another Italian redoubt, then the road descended to Gondar.

The battalion's mortar platoon led by Captain MacFie arrived as we dug in. MacFie, who had attended the Middle East Weapon Training School earlier that year, had brand-new 3-inch mortars. He was very keen to use them. We watched the Italian positions through our field glasses and waited eagerly for MacFie's men to fire. Two dozen or so bombs were duly lobbed at the enemy, raising puffs of smoke on the flanks of Venticinque, provoking some inaccurate return fire which continued sporadically the following day.

On 17 November, the day of the attack, the brigade's 4.5-inch howitzers and 25-pounder field guns bombarded the Italian positions during the afternoon, an accompaniment to an early dinner which we ate on Green Hill at 1530. At 1645 several planes dive-bombed and strafed enemy artillery and mortar positions on Venticinque and neighbouring points. The air attack was followed by mortar fire registered on the same targets. Captain Tidmarsh had established a forward HQ at a captured sentry post in the valley. Two platoons, one from A Company (Second Lieutenant Moncur) and the other from C Company (Lieutenant Sceales), waited nearby. At 1730 they leapt from their start lines and rushed forward. The King's African Rifles gave covering fire. MacFie's mortars popped away adding to the din. The Italians, who had kept their heads down during the initial bombardment, started shooting back. I watched the assault through my field glasses, seeing the tiny figures obscured briefly by a smokescreen from MacFie's mortars as they scrambled up the hill. I was shocked to see Moncur fall as he and his men reached the summit.

Minutes later a breathless runner from Battalion HQ handed me a scrap of paper on which Second Lieutenant Scheurmier, our Intelligence Officer, had pencilled an urgent scrawl:

To Ward: you will proceed direct to Capt. Tidmarsh and take over

Moncur's platoon on hill.

At the briefing that morning I had written out the plan of attack in a field message pad, as I had been taught to do at Dunbar—information, intention, method. All that was immediately chucked as I breenged forward to rescue the leaderless platoon. This was my first chance in action and the order was too exciting for me to feel scared. I sprinted across the valley and dashed up the hill, exhilarated even when bullets from an enemy outpost whistled past my ears as I ran. Bloomfield told me later that my platoon had watched fascinated as I covered the ground in leaps and bounds like a gazelle. Moncur was dead and his platoon demoralised. Daylight was fading. One of the men was shell-shocked. A breeze sprang up, chilling the sweat that had suddenly broken out all over me. I must have been oblivious to the risk. I could have approached the hill more prudently, but I was keen as mustard to prove myself and intoxicated with virility and by the violence. Later, I realised that I was lucky to have survived that first foray and not been a statistic like poor Moncur. Among the brutal certainties of the infantryman's war was that the casualty rate among inexperienced but eager young platoon commanders was high.

The moment Moncur was killed the Italians abandoned Venticinque. They lost a dozen men whose bodies lay crumpled among sandbags, water bottles and cans of sardines. In one gun-pit an Italian soldier was sprawled over the breech of a Breda machine-gun and two others lay dead beside him, all hit by shrapnel that seemed to have left them unmarked. I turned away from that weird tableau and shouted at the men to organise a defensive position because we had orders to remain on Venticinque until 0430 the following morning. We spent an uneasy night, made more so for me by unwelcome orders from Battalion HQ to recce the ridge. I argued with the adjutant about that; said it wasn't necessary because I had seen the 'Eyeties' skedaddle and that I didn't think they would try to retake the position. To no avail, so Sergeant Grant and I scoured the top of the hill. We found only more abandoned equipment and empty slit trenches.

We were relieved by another platoon and returned to Green Hill the next day. That evening there was a skirmish with an Italian patrol somewhere on the ridge. Shots were exchanged, although neither side knew where the other was. There were no Argyll casualties. Lieutenant Oxborrow of A Company reported this activity. The ridge was secured at 0200 by Sceales' platoon. On Green Hill we were woken by a single shot followed by angry shouts in the dark. An investigation into the cause of the rumpus made things clear. Shaw and six men had passed through our lines on a night patrol. On their return a trigger-happy sentry let off a shot that wounded Shaw in the arm. It was only a flesh wound but Shaw was mortified at becoming a casualty in such stupid way. Confusion over the password or the time and place of the patrol's return was the likely cause.

At the end of the week we had a bash in the company commander's tent, my 25th birthday being the excuse. The evening ended with our quartermaster sergeant on his back in front of our position singing and howling obscenities at the Italians. The next morning we struggled to our posts for Stand-to and watched and listened for the enemy who, we were convinced, had heard every word of the drunken abuse and would be insulted enough to attack us. What we heard was unidentified initially. It became a whisper and a rustle, then a swish and a clatter. We exchanged bewildered looks and reached for our weapons. Seconds later a wave of jabbering clamour broke over our position. We ducked as a stream of dark shapes flashed past, leaping and swinging through the bushes and across our trenches, yelping and shrieking like devils . . . then a rustle and a whisper and they vanished as mysteriously as they had come—a colony of baboons on the march.

Staying on Green Hill was a soft introduction for me and the men new to active service. We were dug in and bivouacked in our eyrie commanding views of the peculiar landscape; we had good grub from the company cookhouse, cigarette and beer rations, and a rum issue for the cold nights. There was little chance of encounters with the enemy. Below us, peasants returned and resumed threshing corn. The Italians being attacked from other directions were retreating to Gondar. They surrendered at the end of the month. Two of our officers involved in the negotiations were injured when their truck struck a mine. Landmines were not the only hazard. Bloomfield warned me that a favourite Eyetie trick was to put hands up or wave white flags and, as we lowered our guns, chuck grenades. Fascist swine. Then they would have the cheek to defend points of honour. When Colonel Polverini, the garrison commander on Ambazzo Hill, was invited by Lieutenant Sceales to surrender he announced grandly that he had received no orders from his commander, Lieutenant-General Nasi, to do so. After an exchange of artillery fire he changed his mind and walked into captivity a contented cavalier, honour satisfied. As far as we were concerned there were no honours of war at Ambazzo and Venticinque. At that moment I despised the Italians for killing Moncur, for their vanity, their token resistance and habit of throwing grenades and running away.

Nasi surrendered unconditionally an army of 11,500 Italians and 12,000 askaris, along with 400 machine-guns, dozens of mortars and field guns, and ammunition and small arms. The defeat was the curtain call of Africa Orientale Italiana, the Italian East African empire.

We took part in a victory parade at Gondar. Among the Allied units was a band of Abyssinian irregulars, the Patriots. They wore Italian army boots and bandoliers, and carried machetes and Italian-issue Austro-Hungarian rifles, or weapons supplied by Special Operations Executive (SOE). These 'fuzzy-wuzzies' evidently terrified the Italians we rounded up, disarmed and put in PoW pens. Mussolini's conscripts were a dispirited bunch. His officers were a comfort-loving, haughty lot who smelled not of sweat but of eau-de-cologne. They were dressed immaculately in gold-braid, tailored jackets, riding breeches and leather cavalry boots. The élite Bersaglieri wore cockerel-feathered hats. Not since the most formal occasions at Stirling Castle had I seen such a display of elegant military plumage. They liked their home comforts too, with wines, brandy and toiletries among their personal effects. It was as if we had travelled back to the etiquette and pageantry of previous era—that we were the victors of a nineteenth-century colonial war.

Looting was endemic in the town despite dire warnings against such activity from higher command. It was small-scale among the troops, including the Jocks, large-scale by some senior officers, some of whom (not Argylls) were court-martialled. My platoon was ordered to guard the Gondar branch of the Banca d'Italia from where a cache of Maria Theresa dollars had been stolen. Some remained in the vault. I like to think they dated from the campaign of General Sir Robert Napier who led an expedition from Bombay in 1868 to overthrow, at the Battle of Magdala, an Abyssinian emperor who was holding Europeans hostage. Napier landed 50 kilometres south of Massawa with an Indo-British army of over 13,000 men and 44 elephants to carry mountain guns and supplies, including 500,000 Maria Theresa silver dollars minted in Vienna, the only currency recognised by Abyssinians and Arab traders. But those in the Banca d'Italia were new. SOE had been smuggling in Maria Theresa dollars minted in Bombay to bribe tribal chiefs, and Mussolini had sent one million from Rome for the same purpose.

I didn't get any, but other precious items fell into my lap. Bloomfield, who fought at Sidi Barrani, had no scruples about getting his own back. He'd sidle up: 'Would you like a camera, sir, a typewriter, a gramophone?' I got all three. The resourceful 'Bloomie' then produced a box of Italian opera records. I played those records in tent, bivouac and barrack room throughout the war. I arranged for a platoon photo to be taken on the plinth of an obelisk which commemorated Mussolini's conquest of Abyssinia. The Italian tenure had been short-lived in the span of history. Gondar's landmark was a picturesque and ruinous seventeenth-century castle set among eucalyptus and cedar groves above the town, which I explored with Tidmarsh and Oxborrow. We went on a shooting trip to Lake Tana, which an eighteenth-century Scottish adventurer, James Bruce, had identified as the source of the Blue Nile. We had acquired Italian shotguns and a couple of native guides. We hoped to see hippos, leopards and lions but we only bagged a brace of pigeons.

The battalion was relieved on 5 December and returned to Asmara. We were amazed to find Lieutenant Macalister Hall waiting for us. He had last been seen on Crete where he had been captured. He held us agog in the Officers' Mess when he told of his escape from a PoW camp at Athens. He went over the wall with two Maoris and an English officer, a classical scholar. They baffled German sentries at checkpoints by babbling in Maori and ancient Greek (like three 8th Battalion Argylls who escaped across France in 1940 by speaking Gaelic when challenged). After the group split up, Macalister Hall reached Turkey by boat with some fugitive Greek army officers. The British consul at Smyrna gave him a fake Jewish identity card and a train ticket to Palestine. Three and a half months after escaping he reached Egypt and was awarded an MC for his enterprise.

We stayed only a few days in Asmara before being posted to Khartoum. The road plunged into the Keren gorge where the Italians had held Lieutenant-General Platt's forces during a siege before they lost Asmara and Massawa. The fight at Venticinque seemed a sideshow when I saw that gorge, its shell craters, trenches and battlefield wreckage. We continued through the mountainous country of western Eritrea to Kassala and across the flat deserts of the Sudan: a 1,000-kilometre drive on increasingly rutted tracks and a complete change in climate and topography. Asmara's art deco architecture and the spectacular mountain roads I had taken from Massawa to Gondar faded as quickly as a dream. As for Venticinque, that small battlefield in Abyssinia in 1941 . . . I see it now like the band of baboons sweeping across our camp: a passage that has left no trace. I doubt that any Ethiopian passing Venticinque now either knows of the Argylls or why we were there.

The battalion arrived at Khartoum towards the end of December 1941. One of the things we subalterns had to do there was to write an essay on whether or not, in the light of our recent experience, our training before being commissioned had been suitable. My mind wandered back to Stirling Castle and my strange new life as a soldier. I had few criticisms to offer. When I thought of Abyssinia I found it difficult to remember the dangers and discomforts and chose to recall how happy I was through it all. The camaraderie we enjoyed, the exquisite feeling of freedom, the health and strength we revelled in, and the knowledge that our expedition was worthwhile made an impression greater than all the petty annoyances and fears. I still look back with pleasure and thankfulness on that curious campaign in East Africa.

I had been travelling in a region previously familiar to me only from tales of exploration and empire, or simply as names in a school atlas. Hearing or reading of such places now evokes memories of times spent in foreign lands among strange peoples. We of course were the foreigners and must have appeared as outlandish to the natives as they did to us, never more so than when we marched through Cairo, Asmara, Gondar and Khartoum wearing our kilts, with pipes playing and drums beating.

Khartoum barracks dated from Kitchener's time. It was a broad, dusty compound of verandahed buildings and tents where we enjoyed three months of more or less peacetime soldiering in the style of a past age of imperial power. Drill, desert training and a routine punctuated at regular intervals by bugle calls were the order of the day. Whenever we marched along the Nile promenade to mount guard at the Governor's Palace we passed a bronze statue of General Gordon on a camel. At a Christmas service in the Anglican cathedral we sang carols under whirring ceiling fans. Hogmanay was a traditional bash, followed by a Burns Supper and the Battalion Highland Games. MacDougall, Shaw and I, as visiting officers, were admitted as temporary members to the Sudan Club, a gleaming colonial villa. We dined there occasionally, swam in the pool, played cricket and enjoyed all the privileges of representatives of king and empire. Wicker armchairs were set out on the club's immaculate lawn where we sat often, with lemonade or whisky and soda in the cool of an evening, attended by a trio of white-robed Sudanese who served us with courteous deference. At the club's garden party we were stunned by the spectacle of Khartoum's imperial society looking and talking as if wafted from the pages of P. G. Wodehouse.

One of our training exercises had the whole battalion out on the site of the Battle of Omdurman, where Kitchener's army crushed an Islamic uprising of 1898. Conditions there were excellent for desert warfare training. We were put through assault and obstacle courses or footslogged, aimlessly we thought, in ferocious 100-degree heat. We were given ack-ack training with Brens mounted on tripods. As I found later in the Western Desert, none of us was brave or stupid enough to stand up during an air attack to fire them. In any case, our chances of bringing down an enemy plane required very lucky shots. I never saw one.

In the Officers' Mess some evenings MacDougall, Shaw and I sang popular songs in close harmony to entertain the CO and his second in command as they drank whisky and soda. Evenings always ended with the appearance of the orderly officer of the day, a role at which I took my turn. In full uniform, I would tour the camp at Lights Out, inspect the guards and receive a report from each company sergeant major (CSM), then march back to the mess and declare: 'All companies present and correct, arms and ammo secure, guards counted.' I would be dismissed by the adjutant with a courteous 'Thank you', before going off to bed. I shared a room with padre Smith, a jovial fellow who had been a champion boxer in his student days. He made an effort to know all the men in the battalion and they had great respect for him. One of his duties was to conduct the annual Divine Service, to commemorate the Raising of the Regiment on 10 February 1794. The anniversary service, with its unchanging programme of Kipling's 'Recessional' and the 91st Psalm, was held in the cathedral on Sunday morning, 8 February 1942.

The war seemed far away, especially the fighting in the Far East. We had heard of the Japanese attack on Pearl Harbor when we were in Abyssinia. In Khartoum we got the numbing news that Singapore had fallen. The Argylls' 2nd Battalion was the last unit to cross the causeway from Malaya to Singapore before the surrender to the Japanese. We were back in Egypt by the time we learned of its exploits and fate. Details were obtained by our CO from its commander, Brigadier MacAlister Stewart, and circulated to all ranks. Because of his jungle warfare experience, Stewart, with three other Argyll officers, was flown to GHQ India after the battalion's 53-day rearguard action down the Malayan peninsula. The other survivors became PoWs in Japanese camps and forced labour on the 'death railway' dramatised after the war in *The Bridge on the River Kwai.* My preference for a posting in 1940 had been 2nd Battalion. Bloomfield told me he had arrived at Singapore from India with it in August 1939. Fortunately for him, his overseas tour ended before the attack on Malaya. He was posted to the UK and then to 1st Battalion in Egypt.

Of more immediate concern to us, battles still raged across the Western Desert. We had a visit from a Major Roosevelt, a son of the President of the United States, sent on a fact-finding mission to British Middle East Forces. Our lifestyle no doubt confirmed him in his father's jaundiced views of the British empire, but he was an amiable fellow who took in good part some ragging about America's part in the war. We hoped he'd report back home on our firm belief that the Allies would win it.

We were reinforced with 153 men, two of whom I got to know well, second lieutenants Johnnie Scott-Barrett and George Rome. McGill was transferred to the Trans-Jordan Frontier Force. Lieutenant-Colonel Anderson was promoted to lead the 29th East African Brigade. He was succeeded by Lieutenant-Colonel Ronnie McAlister who took command on 10 April. On 4 May we left Khartoum on a 1,500-kilometre journey to Cairo by single-track railway, river steamer and another train. The Wadi Halfa to Khartoum railway had been completed in 1898 to bypass the Nile rapids and supply Kitchener's army. Our train was the heir to that enterprise. Before the war it was called the Nile Valley Express. Now it was hot, cramped and slow.

'Open the windows!' Shaw gasped, and let in a noxious brew of smoke, cinders and sand.

Pulling down the slatted shutters made the heat worse.

'Try the fans,' I shouted.

They worked. Mac produced a bottle of whisky.

'Courtesy of the Sudan Club,' he grinned.

The railway track ran dead straight for 370 kilometres across the Nubian desert, whose only features were the line of telegraph poles beside the track and infrequent numbered halts where the hissing locomotive took on water. After 15 hours we boarded a rusty paddle steamer at Wadi Halfa. Most of us slept on deck, under the plume of black smoke the steamer trailed as it churned in midstream. For a further 15 hours we saw nothing but the Nile and its desolate hinterland, and occasional mud villages among clusters of palms. Thomas Cook's tourists, for whom the steamer had been built, would have been enchanted by the sunset and sunrise I saw on that passage. At Aswan we collected our kit, tumbled off the ship and marched to the station for a night train to Cairo where we arrived on 13 May.

The battalion was assigned internal security and ceremonial duties: parades for Empire Day, the King's Birthday and Bastille Day, and mounting guard at the British Embassy. B Company, back from Kufra, was based with D Company at the Citadel barracks. MacFie's mortar men were sent to help defend the Delta Barrage, a dam that controlled floodwaters on the Nile. Another platoon was flown on a brief adventure behind enemy lines to guard a secret desert airstrip. A and C companies were ordered to Alex for security duty, patrolling the docks on the lookout for parachutists and saboteurs. These threats were taken seriously. A few months earlier, Italian frogmen on mini-submarines had fixed limpet mines to two Royal Navy battleships which sank when the mines went off. As the harbour was only three fathoms deep, the warships were refloated but spent two months in dry dock. The present danger, however, was not frogmen. It came from the Western Desert where the Afrika Korps was on the offensive.

4 The Perfect Battlefield

The first soldier I spotted in the Western Desert was a military policeman standing in a swirl of dust outside Alexandria, shouting at the traffic: 'Get a move on. We haven't got all bloody day!' Trucks packed with dead-eyed troops were retreating from the front and others, including mine, with wide-eyed innocents were heading for it. The road forked where the MP stood. I remember two signs: 'Alexandria, 7 kilos' and 'To the Western Desert'. No distance was given to the desert. It was there, vast and empty except for drifting dust clouds that might be sandstorms, or stirred up by the jousting armies out 'in the blue' as we called it.

My first duty in the desert I am sure every infantryman who served in the Eighth Army remembered: I dug trenches, lots of them. While fluid tank engagements had characterised the battles of 1941–1942, the foot soldier's experience in the desert was more like the First World War. My company was set to work with 100 Indian pioneers digging communications trenches and field-gun positions behind a minefield, part of defences being organised hastily in case the Alamein line was pierced by the Afrika Korps. After Wavell had crushed the Italians at Sidi Barrani in December 1940 the front line had swayed to and fro across the Egyptian frontier with Libya, then an Italian colony. Subsequently, each side attacked and counter-attacked, neither gaining a conclusive advantage, although it looked as if Rommel, the Afrika Korps commander, might have one now. Tobruk had just fallen, a shambles that even Cairo's censors couldn't conceal. The garrison of over 33,000, including the Worcesters, had to surrender. The Eighth Army retreated over 500 kilometres in 11 days. On 1 July 1942 General Auchinleck made a stand at El Alamein, a desert railway halt only a couple of hours from Alex and Cairo.

The presence of the Afrika Korps at El Alamein spread alarm and confusion. The cities and the Suez Canal were vital to the war effort and to the security of the Middle East and the Gulf oilfields. Fifth columnists and enemy parachutists were rumoured to be everywhere. Curfews were imposed. In Alex I recall being told to carry my service revolver at all times. The navy prepared to leave. The docks were mined for demolition to prevent their use by the enemy. In Cairo the Embassy was besieged for exit visas; there was a run on the banks; railway stations and shipping offices were swamped with evacuees desperate for tickets.

Out in the blue we were on edge most of the time as we dug defences, not knowing Rommel's intentions or where or when the enemy would strike. At the end of July there was a lull as the armies disengaged. Like everyone in the Eighth Army that month I remember being showered with orders, counter-orders and false alarms. We were pulled back on 15 August to Amiriya, having seen no real action. Amiriya was a transit camp for troops moving from Alex and Cairo to and from the Western Desert. Accommodation was in trenches or tents. There were no amenities apart from occasional Naafi trucks. Despite the organisation's motto, 'Service to the Services', these usually ran out of goodies just as you got to them. Tanks rolled by stirring up clouds of dust; salt lakes added a sting to the air and eyes. Infantrymen from the front mooched around brewing tea while they waited for orders. At casualty stations marked by Red Cross flags stretcher cases lay under makeshift canvas shelters.

The battalion camped in an olive grove from which an Arab family squeezed a scant living. We were deployed for airfield defence. The Desert Air Force (DAF: the RAF and Allied air forces in Egypt) had lost its forward landing grounds and regrouped at Amiriya. The airstrips had been bulldozed out of the desert and had no infrastructure apart from tents and sandbagged blast pens. Only the dust trails of aircraft taking off or landing, the sound of engines racing and the glow of recognition flares during night operations indicated where the landing grounds were. Air-raid sirens went off all the time. I saw two Messerschmitt 109s scudding over, low enough to see the black crosses on their wings, followed by ack-ack fire which missed them. Occasionally, and often silently, the blazing smoke trail of a downed plane would end in a distant eruption of sand or a white plume on the sea. The sky over Alex at night was criss-crossed by searchlight beams. We were jumpy because we had been told to watch for German paratroops, but rumours of their landings were unfounded. After losses on Crete German paratroop divisions were used mainly as ground forces. They were still feared and respected. The Argylls would get to know them again, in Italy.

The 'flap' in July prompted Churchill to fly to Cairo with the Chief of the Imperial General Staff, General Sir Alan Brooke, to reorganise Middle East Command. They arrived on 3 August. Churchill sacked Auchinleck, as he had Wavell. The new Commander-in-Chief Middle East was General Sir Harold Alexander, untainted by Tobruk or the retreat to El Alamein. The Eighth Army's new commander was Lieutenant-General Bernard Law Montgomery. He landed in Egypt on 12 August and visited Auchinleck's forward HQ which he found unsatisfactory. He moved it from Ruweisat Ridge to the coastal sand dunes at Burg el Arab, where Eighth Army and Desert Air Force headquarters were now located and where he could co-ordinate tactical air support for the army. He replaced the static forward HQ with Tactical Headquarters (Tac HQ), a mobile unit to be deployed near the front line. The Argylls were apparently among the units being considered to guard it.

Captain Tidmarsh gave me the gen from Battalion HQ. My platoon had been chosen for a dummy run on 22 August. We gobbled breakfast amid much speculation, then loaded kit, weapons and ammo (less tents, since it would be a one-day exercise) into four trucks and set off for the rendezvous at kilometre 20 on the Alex to Cairo road. We arrived at 0900. In charge was Major Oswald, G2 (general staff officer, grade two, opera-tions) with Major Andrews of the Seaforths. I was briefed briskly for the 'bodyguard exercise'. Oswald had a couple of dozen vehicles and a colour-ful crew of officers and men. These were Tac HQ brass, liaison officers, signalmen, tank crews and ack-ack chaps, all assigned a role or, like 9 Platoon, A Company, the Argylls, being assessed for one. We spent the full day out in the blue practising map reading, manoeuvres, formation driving, setting up laagers and ack-ack dispersal. Because radio silence was often necessary flag signals had to be learned. Thus I was initiated into the craft of desert travel. We got a lot of it over the next four months, before and after the decisive Battle of El Alamein. I made diary notes (which inform much of this text), against regulations because it was forbidden to keep a diary when in close contact with the enemy.

I saw Montgomery for the first time when we were passing a line of stationary vehicles on the coast road the day after the exercise. He was standing in an open-top Humber staff car, his arms leaning on the windscreen as he scanned the horizon, like a hawk looking for quarry. In shirtsleeves, beret and holding a fly whisk he looked unconventional with no obvious brass. I took a quick photo. He was visiting troops, dishing out cigarettes, full of confidence and bonhomie. A few days later Alexander, accompanied by corps, division and brigade brass hats, inspected the battalion. I met him briefly, a former Irish Guards officer, armed with a revolver and aristocratic charm, dressed in breeches, high boots, sheepskin-lined jacket, medal-ribboned tunic and red-banded cap. Alexander and his gang were upbeat, already in the Monty mould. Bloomfield doubted if Rommel would be bothered. The Afrika Korps leader had acquired a legendary status among us as well as with his own soldiers. Even in deepest Abyssinia, reports of the 'Desert Fox' and his exploits had reached us. He favoured fast-moving warfare and had better weapons, particularly tanks and the 88mm flak gun which the Afrika Korps used as an anti-tank gun to devastating effect.

Before Monty arrived the German commander was probably the Eighth Army's most popular general. I certainly felt that our morale and self-esteem were boosted by the knowledge that we were fighting a daring and honourable enemy. He had a reputation for fair play that virtually guaranteed him the respect of the British officer class. Perhaps we forgot about the régime he served. We didn't call Rommel or his men Nazis, just 'Jerries'. They called us 'Tommies' or 'Jocks'. Lest this seem too chummy for men who were trained and sometimes required to kill each other and who often died horribly, I think most of us wanted to believe some decency could survive the absurdity, chaos and cruelty of war; indeed, many veterans of the fighting found the myths that embellish the campaign more comforting than the often grim reality. For men on both sides, the desert seemed a greater enemy. It stripped everything to essentials. We were alone far from home fighting a private war. There was no civilian population to complicate the contest. For both armies the Western Desert was a perfect battlefield.

The Desert War was confined to an 800-kilometre-long, limestone coastal plateau no higher than 200 metres above sea level; a landscape of flat sand, loose stones, rocky low ridges and shallow wadis, with none of the photogenic sand dunes seen in the film *Lawrence of Arabia*. Scattered settlements, the two-lane coast road, and the Alex to Mersa Matruh railway built by the British in the 1920s, ran along a sea-level coastal strip no more than a few kilometres wide. At El Alamein the plateau was only 60 kilometres wide, squeezed between the Mediterranean coast and the Qattara Depression, a dried-up sea bed 120 metres below sea level, covered with salt and shifting sand all but impassable to vehicles. With the Mediterranean to the north and a southern flank which could not be turned easily the Afrika Korps and the Eighth Army were forced to confront each other on the Alamein line, to which Auchinleck had fallen back knowing it was the narrowest defensive position before Alex and Cairo. To proceed, Rommel would have to make either a head-on attack along the coast or attempt a flanking manoeuvre to the south. Two low ridges, Ruweisat and Alam Halfa, helped secure the flank.

At the end of August the Argylls were ordered to join 161 Brigade, 5th Indian Division on Ruweisat Ridge where we relieved the exhausted and depleted 1/2nd Punjabis. As this was likely to be an extended tour on the front line I assembled my platoon and verified each man's name, age, rank, religion, army and rifle serial numbers, height and size of boots, and checked each wore his dog tag. Most of the 30 men were from the west of Scotland. Apart from Sanders and Bloomfield only two were over 30; a few were regular army, a few were volunteers; two-thirds had been drafted; most were under 25 and most gave their mothers as next of kin. They represented a cross section of the skilled and unskilled prewar working class, from shipyard riveters to farm labourers. That roll call had a biblical resonance as they stood in front of me and confirmed who and what they were. One-third of those Jocks had been unemployed before joining up—the poor bloody infantry in more ways than one.

The desert seemed to swallow all that entered it. We learned how to navigate like sailors, by the sun and stars. We had maps, but apart from the coastline, the road and railway there was little on them except low ridges and the Qattara Depression. Rendezvous was by a six-figure map reference within numbered military zones. The map references corresponded to numbered Field Survey oil drums, painted white and anchored like mooring buoys on desert tracks, when you could find them that is, the drums or the tracks. Tracked vehicles like Bren carriers could ride the terrain. Metal sand mats and shovels were used to unstick trucks. The sand crust could give way and a plunge at speed into a hidden wadi would take the axles off. Broken axles, boiling radiators, sand in the carburettors, burst tyres . . . I became familiar with them all. Our moves in the months before Alamein were across country or on well-worn tracks, often through swirling clouds of dust churned up by tanks and heavy vehicles. Bad enough when we were vehicle-borne, worse when marching on foot.

Ruweisat Ridge on which we were deployed was a desolate, lizard-like feature. Its western tip, the scene of fierce battles not long before, was a graveyard of burned-out tanks, ours and Jerry's. We stood-to every dawn and dusk for enemy attacks; we were placed on stand-by, then stood down as orders came and went; we changed positions to rotate with other units in our brigade. That was partly operational, but also because many senior officers had been in the trenches in the First World War and understood there was a limit to men's endurance on the front line. It was a restless life never long in the same place, accepting as cheerfully as we could our lot in higher command's scheme of things.

The first shock I experienced on the desert front line was the complete absence of four things normally taken for granted: freedom of movement; secure shelter; decent food; clean water. Slit trenches hardly qualified, nor sangars (shallow holes piled with a semicircle of stones). They gave some protection from enemy fire but no relief from the blazing sun or the night chill. Dugouts were more substantial, being protected by sandbags and covered with sheets of corrugated iron. Inside these hovels, with mosquito netting and canvas draped across the entrances, we slept like troglodytes on shelves cut out of the sand. Not that we always slept much or easily; we were frequently disturbed by bursts of shellfire. Cooking fires and lights were restricted and the tell-tale glow from cigarettes was concealed by cupped hands. In the midday sun, temperatures were often high enough to fry eggs on truck bonnets, which we did for a laugh. Not often: the risk of being shelled or machine-gunned more or less confined us to our holes until dusk.

From the first day on the ridge, artillery fire, ours and theirs, swished over our heads to explode elsewhere. Some shells came closer, forcing us to stay in our holes where we would lie, petrified, shaken by the concussion and peppered by shrapnel. When it was safe to raise our heads to see if we were all okay we tried to appear completely unconcerned about the stonk. I noted how experienced officers casually ignored shells bursting nearby and steeled myself to copy their composure under fire, a most difficult pose to maintain. Green Hill in Abyssinia aside, this was my first sustained experience of frontline soldiering. I had not even been bombed. That soon changed. Ruweisat Ridge was easily spotted from the air and it attracted Stukas like flies.

We were often dive-bombed at teatime: 1730. You could set your watch by those nuisance raids and we got used to them. But I will never forget the first time I was a Stuka target. Bloomfield yelled: 'Get down!' and jumped into a foxhole. I leapt in after him and curled up in a ball, sand and rock an inch from my face. I dared to look up. Just when I thought the plane would hit the ground, the pilot released a 500-kilogramme bomb and pulled up and away. The black crosses on the wings seemed particularly malevolent at that moment, as did the falling bomb. This all seemed to happen in slow motion, until the bomb screamed down and burst with a deafening crash and an eruption of rock and sand; then silence, except for the fallout of sand and pebbles pattering our position like rain. I looked around to check the number of tin hats that appeared from our holes as the smoke and dust blew away and shouted, 'Everyone okay?' No casualties. Unless the bomb scored a direct hit, or shrapnel caught you in the open, it could land less than 100 metres away and you'd be shaken but you would survive.

The longer we stayed in the desert the more we became prisoners of the pervasive normality of it all, as if no other life were possible. Every patrol, every move we made, unless forced by the urgency of the battlefield, was typed out methodically in advance at Battalion or Company HQ. A dispatch rider or runner would hand me a 'secret' envelope. I'd unfold sheets of paper, typical of the bureaucracy of war, for yet another patrol, usually at night. Task: 'Act offensively and obtain enemy prisoners or identification as opportunity offers and report on position and type of enemy dispositions.' These instructions became routine but the patrols, by platoon or section, were always tense. We would blacken our faces, pull on balaclavas, suede desert boots, and pullovers to keep out the cold. Equipment wasn't carried except for small arms, ammo and compasses. I have never forgotten leading those men all similarly keyed-up out through gaps in the wire, then fanning out in arrowhead formation over rough ground scattered with unexpected obstacles and shallow depressions: the grip of fear, of bumping into an enemy patrol or stepping on mines or tripwires; keeping silent, keeping distance, keeping alert, straining eyes and ears not knowing what to expect; lying motionless flat on the sand to listen for voices, movement, the sound of a rifle bolt; the night sky lit with stars, flashes of tracer and artillery fire and flares like fireworks burning as they fell. There was an eerie beauty to it all.

One night we were shelled by our own artillery. Back through the wire I grabbed a couple of hours sleep, then was pestered all morning by gunners and intelligence officers about the effect of the harassing shoot which we had witnessed and came close to being caught up in. I told them that next time they might consider harassing Jerry. On another occasion our IO (intelligence officer) wanted a prisoner. Bloomfield and I went out alone and managed to worm our way among enemy work parties. We heard the Jerries talking as we waited like cats to ambush a straggler. To be frank, we were relieved that none of the Jerries came our way. I still wonder what we'd have done if we'd met an armed patrol. Shoot, surrender, run like hell? We preferred to avoid surprise encounters and I'm sure Jerry felt the same.

On parts of the ridge it was safe to patrol in daylight. On one such recce Bloomie and I took a 15-cwt truck 2,500 yards into no-man's-land. Dust began to blow and we didn't see much. We had to dig ourselves out when the truck got stuck in soft sand, which caused momentary panic when I realised we had lost our bearings. Later, we came across the grotesque, wind-blown sight of three skeletons of half-buried Indian Sepoys, their eyeless skulls gazing at the sky. We covered them up as best we could and I offered up a silent prayer for those poor fellows killed so far from home.

We had an odd intimacy with the enemy, the sense that in our lonely battlefield friend and foe shared the same fate. It was sometimes hard to tell the two sides apart. Each captured the other's rations, transport, equipment and clothing, causing occasional confusion on the battlefield. Nothing was wasted. The Germans drove captured trucks and ate our rations (canned South African peaches apparently being preferred). We were partial to Italian food and wine. We prized Jerry's 20-litre, steel petrol containers. These 'Jerrycans' were more robust than our Egyptian-made four-gallon tins which leaked from shoddy welding. Unfit as they were for purpose, ours proved ideal as kettles or cookers: slice off the top, puncture the sides with a bayonet and pour in a sand and petrol mixture which would burn for about half an hour, over which a tin with a wire handle could be suspended and filled with water—perfect for a morale-boosting brew-up. If Jerry had somehow found a way to deprive us of tea, or for that matter beer and whisky, we'd have lost the war in a week. Water was rationed to four to six pints per day per man, brought up by truck from B Echelon at night. It always tasted brackish or chlorinated, or had been in petrol tins. Half was for cooking and tea, half for a wash and shave. Any left went into vehicle radiators. We were brought one hot meal a day, M & V (an unvarying meat and vegetable stew) from the cook's truck at night; otherwise bully beef and hardtack. Those biscuits were more palatable soaked in sugar and condensed milk, a concoction that attracted flies. I rarely complained about food after the war. Flies covered everything, penetrated everywhere, breeding in latrines and on corpses. The dead were buried quickly if conditions allowed.

Desert life had its lighter moments. There were quiet days with no artillery or air activity. On such evenings we'd follow dials (arrows of stones) or compass bearings, or pace out the distance in the dark to each other's positions for beer, whisky and chat. What we'd have done without the stimulating and restorative qualities of alcohol in our circumstances I don't know. The regular beer ration did the same for the men. Bloomfield was in the habit of carousing with his crony, the Company Quartermaster Sergeant, and often returned late and half fu'. He'd wake me up by blundering into our covered dugout muttering, 'Duck the heid, Bloomie, duck the heid.' Thereafter, whenever the platoon was dive-bombed or shelled we took to yelling 'Duck the heid, Bloomie' as we scrambled for cover.

Eccentric behaviour was normal. I caught a chameleon and kept it on a string to catch flies. We would shake our boots in the mornings to expel scorpions. I took postal singing lessons from my father with the intention of becoming a professional singer after the war. I roped in Sanders and am now struck by the absurdity of walking around with a music score singing with my batman in the desert. All of us tuned into the BBC when our radios weren't set for artillery shoots or army communications. We would pick up the Afrika Korps signal and hear 'Lili Marlene', the haunting melody which captivated soldiers on both sides. Non-standard dress was common. Soft desert boots ('brothel-creepers' we called them) were more comfortable than the regular army issue and an essential part of an Eighth Army officer's image. A craft industry sprang up in the backstreets of Cairo to satisfy the demand for them. The classic outfit was the ankle-high suede boots, shorts or corduroy trousers, wool or cotton pullovers, silk scarves and sheepskin jackets. The style, modelled by Monty no less, was lampooned affectionately in 'The Two Types' cartoons penned by

Captain W. J. P. Jones of the Army Newspaper Unit.

We read avidly and discussed current affairs. In my experience the men were politically aware. In officers' messes throughout my active service many arguments and discussions ensued, serious and light-hearted. Copies of the *Egyptian Mail* and *Eighth Army News* circulated until they disintegrated or were used as lavatory paper. Whenever I went to Alex or Cairo I brought back reading matter for me and the men. I recall Mac and Shaw in my dugout where we read snatches of *Henry V* aloud to each other on off-duty evenings, identifying with the play's themes of bravery and brotherhood in arms. I got to know some South African and New Zealand fellows among the anti-tank and ack-ack crews in our sector, who shared their cigarettes, Canadian Club whisky and chocolate. There was a tremendous spirit among all of us despite our grumbles about our monotonous diet, the cold nights, the heat, dust and flies. Away from the front lines the desert was clean and clear, a purifying austerity. Cool breezes tempered the heat and dispersed the flies. The sun and stars produced magical effects. Then nature would play its tricks, with mirages of Jerry tanks or furious sandstorms. We had no defence against sandstorms and not much against the panzers.

The bizarre thing about our situation, apart from the spectacle of nature's mocking beauty and brutality, was that the pleasures of Alex and Cairo were only a couple of hours drive away. In this respect we were better off than the enemy soldiers who were days away from Benghazi and Tripoli. Leave offered a temporary return to comfort and sanity. The prospect of it produced fantasies of real beds and hot baths at Shepheard's and being groomed by Cairo's attentive barbers; or swimming at Stanley Bay and flirting with girls on the Corniche, and of ice cold lager at the Cecil and decent food at the Union Club . . . But every time I headed back up the blue, seeing the familiar 'To the Western Desert' sign on the Alex to Cairo highway, I always felt a heightened sense that I was young, fit and alive. Grains of sand stick to me still, such was the effect of the desert and the nomadic life and camaraderie I found there.

5 Monty's Bodyguard

Montgomery expected Rommel to attack before the Eighth Army was reinforced and re-equipped. The Afrika Korps and its attached Italian divisions were at the limit of their supply chain from Benghazi and Tobruk to El Alamein. It was thought (not by us in our dugouts at the time, but evident later) that Rommel would avoid the coastal sector at El Alamein and make a flanking thrust south of Ruweisat Ridge. His army could then turn north to the coast road, cut off the Eighth Army and strike swiftly to Alex, Cairo and the Delta. To secure a passage he would have to capture Alam Halfa Ridge to the south of us. Alam Halfa bristled with anti-tank guns, artillery and hull-down tanks to stop the panzers, which also risked exposure to the Desert Air Force. Rommel would be halted and the final battle at El Alamein fought.

One of Monty's gifts was to make every man know why he was fighting, what was expected of him and that the general relied on him. He would stand on a Jeep and talk to hundreds of men, making each one feel that his individual conduct mattered. Even those who never saw one of those performances felt his presence, by word of mouth, from pictures and quotes in the Eighth Army's newspapers and from each 'Personal Message from the Army Commander' printed before every battle and handed or read to every man. Monty ordered the armoured divisions to stop 'swanning about in the desert' in disorganised deployments. Rommel's attacks had punched through these easily in previous engagements. He tore up GHQ's plans for retreat and transformed the Eighth Army from a dispirited and confused miscellany into a confident, unified, battle-winning force.

Orders of the Day were distributed on 30 August:

TO OFFICERS AND MEN OF THE EIGHTH ARMY
SPECIAL MESSAGE.

The enemy is now attempting to break through our positions in order to reach CAIRO, SUEZ, and ALEXANDRIA, and to drive us from EGYPT. The Eighth Army bars the way. It carries a great responsibility and the whole future of the war will depend on how we carry out our task. We will fight the enemy where we now stand; there will be NO WITHDRAWAL and NO SURRENDER.

Rommel attacked that night in what became known as the Battle of Alam Halfa. We were ready to move at a moment's notice, to march anywhere in the brigade area and counter-attack. Battle Order: steel helmets, shorts, boots, puttees; all weapons carried, mortar bombs, grenades, Bren and tommy guns, spare magazines. But we only played a supporting role, patrolling at night and sticking to our dugouts, slit trenches and sangars anticipating attacks by day. We were shelled routinely and bombed several times but saw no enemy tanks during the battle which lasted five days. I remember hearing heavy gunfire from the south and seeing flares and explosions from midnight until dawn on the first night. No casualties in our area, but rumours and reports told of heavy fighting and air activity elsewhere. There was plenty of ack-ack and we witnessed many aerial dogfights, Hurricanes and 109s or Stukas. Three planes were shot down and one pilot bailed out over our sector on the day before the battle. There were beautiful cloud effects, a majestic backdrop to a swift fight between puny mortals.

Rommel received a bloody nose at the battle, after which the front line reverted to a temporary stalemate. Captain Tidmarsh, Sanders and others went on six days' leave to Alex leaving me in charge as acting Company Commander. I was promoted to full lieutenant and felt tremendously important as OC (Officer Commanding) A Company for what turned out to be an eventful week. Shaw heard about Captain McFie and D Company's role in a raid on Tobruk (the Argylls were not landed but were bombed at sea on the way back to Alex). I was dive-bombed at Battalion HQ, then C Company was shelled by our own artillery. My platoons laid wire and mines at forward positions and continued to patrol along the edge of the ridge. One of my sergeants belly-ached about short rations. Another refused to go on patrol. He had won a Military Medal on Crete so may well have been justified in thinking he'd done his bit, but he wouldn't change his mind despite pleas and threats from the Company Sergeant Major and Bloomfield. That was not an isolated case. Earlier, another of my section leaders shot himself in the foot, accidentally while cleaning his rifle he protested. If the man wasn't malingering he was evidently careless with weapons and a danger to the rest of us. I think he was court-martialled; the other was referred to the Battalion CO and reduced to the ranks. I was disgusted and angry with both wretched cases. Discipline had to be maintained. I couldn't have let either man off the hook even if I'd wanted to.

When Captain Tidmarsh returned I got six days leave, my first for three months, to Cairo with some Jocks who sat on bare boards in the back of the truck singing as we left the ridge. We were in fine fettle as we passed the Pyramids and crossed the Nile to the city where we split up. At Shepheard's, officers swanned about as usual but there was optimism in the air. Rommel had shot his bolt and preparations were going ahead for our big offensive. On the drive back to the blue the macadam hummed with military traffic: staff cars, Jeeps, armoured cars, and trucks loaded with camouflage netting and ammo; convoys of petrol and water tankers and quad tractors towing 25-pounders; transporters loaded with brand-new Sherman tanks (Grant and Sherman tanks shipped from the US and our 25-pounder field guns brought much-needed firepower to the Eighth Army's arsenal). Cheery troops packed into trucks we overtook gave us the thumbs up.

The battalion was resting behind the lines on Ruweisat Ridge. Shortly after I got back Captain Tidmarsh called me to Company HQ.

'Ray! You won't believe this,' he said, handing me a sheet of orders: SPECIAL MISSION. MOST SECRET. Report to General Staff Dept., Main Eighth Army. GOC (Army Commander) Bodyguard.

'Monty's bodyguard?'

'You leave tomorrow. Keep it under your hat.'

A Company's 9 Platoon which I still commanded had been selected as Infantry Guard at Eighth Army Tactical HQ, Monty's mobile command.

I assumed that the day we went swanning around with Major Oswald in August got us the job, and perhaps because my week as temporary OC, A Company had passed without disaster. I read the orders again and briefed Sanders, who was the platoon runner and back-up radio operator as well as my batman, and Bloomfield about our assignment and preparations required. I was excited if not entirely happy about again leaving the battalion and my friends. But at Tac HQ there would be novelty, more responsibility, better food, cooler weather by the sea and fewer flies. That night at Company HQ, Ted, Mac and Shaw laid on a bit of a party for 'Monty's bodyguard'. My diary entry that day ends with me 'rolling home by the light o' the moon'.

On the morning of 2 October I assembled the platoon. Bloomfield appeared smartly with my list of equipment and ordnance and he and I checked each section. Then we all stood around grinning and armed to the teeth, waiting for transport to Burg-el-Arab for our special mission.

Tac HQ was a compact unit formed to enable Monty to conduct the forthcoming offensive from the battlefront, not from GHQ Cairo or some other safe position behind the lines. As a result unit commanders were kept on their toes always half-expecting the army commander to turn up at the front to see things for himself, as indeed he did often. As the Infantry Guard Commander I was responsible for round-the-clock security: identity checks and admittance or refusal to visitors; traffic management and vehicle dispersal; marking the route from the nearest corps to Tac HQ and other signage; camouflage, sentries, trench digging and infantry defence. These tasks were repeated each time Tac HQ moved and a new camp set up as the army advanced.

I noted and got to know the unit's composition:

General Montgomery, his batman, staff and liaison officers; cipher and signals staff, drivers, mechanics, an electrician, cook and orderlies (12 officers and 70 other ranks).

Transport: Armoured Command Vehicle (ACV) plus Monty's personal caravan; five staff cars, seven Bantams (American 4 x 4s, similar to the Jeep) and 15 trucks (five for communications).

Defence: Tank Protective Detachment, B Squadron, 6th Royal Tank Regiment (10 Grant tanks, seven officers, 43 other ranks); 6th South African (two armoured cars, one officer, seven ORs); 1st Armoured Light Aid Detachment workshop (13 ORs); D Troop, 113 Light Anti-Aircraft Battery, Royal Artillery (six Bofors ack-ack guns, tow-trucks, one officer and 40 ORs); Infantry Guard, 9 Platoon, A Company, 1st Argyll and Sutherland Highlanders (one officer and 32 ORs, four platoon trucks).

The ACV was a customised, armour-plated truck with signals staff inside controlling the army's radio communications. It was the Eighth Army's nerve centre in the field, Monty's initiative. His private caravan had a wood-panelled study and map room with, it was said, a picture of Rommel on the wall. I never saw it. The closest I got was posting sentries outside. Major Oswald, to whom I reported, made it clear that Monty detested interruption and I was ordered to refuse entry to anyone arriving at Tac HQ without authorisation, other than his Chief of Staff, Freddie de Guingand, and a handful of divisional and air force commanders. The C-in-C, General Alexander, visited Tac HQ rarely, preferring to leave Monty to plan and direct the action without GHQ's interference.

I got to know Monty's staff and liaison officers. I expected them to be foppish cavalry types (the aide-de-camp, Captain Poston, was an officer in the 11th Hussars). But they were delightful fellows, young, handsome and confident. Pampered too. They had their own mess and bar, which was undisturbed by Monty's aversion to alcohol and tobacco; they had mobile showers, camp beds, sheets, pyjamas, changes of clothes, good food and servants. All had been hand-picked by Monty, his 'boy scouts' Bloomfield called them. Each morning they drove off in their Bantams to liaise with frontline units, reporting back at sunset for debriefing and dinner. In the evenings Monty relaxed in his mess tent. I'd hear bursts of laughter ripple out into the night air while my men and I patrolled the camp perimeter. Monty, a stickler for discipline in most other ways, wore khaki trousers, pullovers and unconventional hats. He sported an Aussie bush hat that glittered with the badges he pinned on each time he visited a different regiment. After taking possession of his personal Grant tank he took to wearing an RTR beret, adding his general's badge to it. Like the bush hat, the beret became a trademark. So did the tank, referred to as 'the army commander's charger'.

Such language might have come from the Light Brigade but Major Coulson, OC the RTR detachment, was a realist. He showed me round one of the Grants. They were death-traps when hit, 'brew-ups' he said and he didn't mean tea. I envied the courage of the 'tankies' but not their occupation, which was dangerous and claustrophobic. Coulson was a fine chap and very kind and helpful to us. I took part in dress rehearsals for Tac HQ on the move, manoeuvring with RTR out in the blue, in a scout car one day after the platoon truck conked out. We recce'd a new position near El Alamein, close to the front line. The weather turned colder at night, followed by heavy dew and thick mist in the mornings. I managed a day in Alex where I lunched at Union Club, went shopping, saw a film and met three RTR blokes at the Cecil Hotel for a few drinks.

Major Oswald, in charge of Tac HQ's organisation, was frank about the forthcoming battle, for which Montgomery had finalised a plan:

Zero Hour: 2200 Friday 23 October; artillery: 800 guns (4.5 inch, 5.5 inch and 25-pounders) for half an hour; mine-lifting and attacks all along the front.

Main attack in the north: 9th Australian, 51st Highland, 2nd New Zealand and 1st South African divisions to break through and establish a bridgehead; 10 Corps tanks then pass through. Diversion in centre by 4th Indian Division; attacks in the south by 50th and 44th divisions, 7th Armoured Division and the Free French Brigade.

Intention: to destroy the enemy in North Africa.

Phase 1. Artillery and aerial bombardment. 2. Infantry attacks establish bridgehead. 3. Infantry pushes on to objectives, mopping up and tanks pass through. 4. Tank battle.

Simple on paper. Not quite what happened.

All through the day on 23 October our thoughts anticipated the artillery barrage that would start the Battle of El Alamein. Montgomery visited our mess during tea. Wiry, keen-eyed, incisive, cheerful, he looked very confident. I had a chat with Lieutenant-General Leese, commanding 30 Corps who, on a frontline tour some weeks before, had inspected A Company's position. He was a bluff, good-humoured, let's-have-a-crack-at-Jerry type. He handed me a printed sheet of paper and told me to read the text to my men. The message was read by or spoken to every soldier in the Eighth Army:

EIGHTH ARMY PERSONAL MESSAGE FROM THE ARMY COMMANDER.

When I assumed command of the Eighth Army I said that the mandate was to destroy ROMMEL and his Army, and that it would be done as soon as we were ready.

We are ready NOW. The battle which is now about to begin will be one of the decisive battles of history. It will be the turning point of the war. The eyes of the whole world will be on us, watching anxiously which way the battle will swing. We can give them their answer at once, 'It will swing our way' . . . there can be only one result: together we will hit the enemy for 'six' right out of North Africa . . .

A full moon rose. I thought of all the poor devils in the infantry lying up all day in the heat and discomfort of their slit trenches, keyed up for the greatest trial of their lives. In the silence you could hear your heartbeat, or was it the ticking of the wrist-watches we kept our eyes on?

2140. 23 October 1942.

The guns started dead on time all along the 20-kilometre front. I watched the fireworks from a vantage point near Tac HQ with Bloomfield and Lieutenant-General Leese. The horizon erupted with artillery flashes. Even at some distance, the noise was thunderous and the ground fairly shook under our feet. Over the racket, Leese, breathing fire like an old warhorse, turned to Bloomfield.

'Don't you wish you were up there at the front, Sergeant?' he bellowed over the din.

Bloomie, no doubt with memories in his mind of Sidi Barrani and Crete, disappointed him by answering sturdily and honestly.

'No, sir.'

Leese didn't ask me. I would have had to answer, 'Yes indeed, sir,' and not admit I was as happy as Bloomie to be where we were, with the brass hats, the usual spectators.

At 2155 the bombardment stopped as abruptly as it had started. I watched tanks move up the road for the breakthrough. Waves of aircraft screamed over to lay smoke and bomb enemy batteries and communications. During this commotion several transporters carrying new Grants for the RTR lumbered into camp unannounced, alarming my sentries. Bloomfield and I dashed to the dispersal area to sort things out. A second barrage continued until 0300. Later, we toasted A Company and the Argylls. There was heavy dew when I crawled into my tent. I slept fitfully and had horrid dreams. Sanders missed the opening salvoes because he'd been away sick but returned the next morning.

Alexander and his Chief-of-Staff, General McCreery, arrived mid-morning from Cairo. In the early hours of the following day Leese and Major-General Lumsden (10th Corps) were led into the camp by de Guingand for an urgent Army Commander's conference, their tension not just the result of a Jerry air raid when they arrived. It was evident the battle was not going according to plan. Vague communiqués were issued and rumours circulated, my only gist of what was going on. In my diary I noted: 7th Armoured Division in the south encountering greater opposition than expected at second minefield . . . success in the north where the main attack is . . . Infantry divisions of 30 Corps gained second objectives and 10 Corps establishing itself in appointed positions . . .

The situation was obscure, with bombing at night and plenty of air activity by day and fierce fighting in the battle area. Two 10th Hussars arrived with Ritter von Thoma, an Afrika Korps general they had captured in no-man's-land. Monty insisted the exhausted Jerry dine with him. I had fresh bread, butter and honey for tea in the RTR mess, occupied myself visiting sentries, checked up on discipline, and swam in the sea some days. I heard that 50 Jerry tanks were knocked out on the 27th. Everything was going satisfactorily it seemed, with the probability of a big tank battle. My duties eased a bit, or so I thought, until one of my sentries was caught asleep at his post by one of Monty's staff officers. Bad show. I got a bit of a rocket at the ACV, then gave my NCOs stick, told them to tighten things up. Major Coulson tried the sentry who got off lightly, with 28 days' field punishment at Amiriya after I intervened. I was cheered up by mail which caught up with us. All well at home, I read, and that my brother Cecil was now in the Royal Marines.

A week after the battle began, Bloomfield and I took a truck and set off in search of the Argylls. We found them not far away, between El Alamein and Ruweisat Ridge. They had been dug-in with the 4th Indian Division. Attacks were ordered, then cancelled when it was clear that the enemy was retreating. Apart from PoWs they saw no enemy. Some time later, I was told that when the battalion did push forward the CO was nearly killed and his driver wounded when their Jeep ran over a Teller mine. A Bren carrier was destroyed in the same way and six men wounded. When the battalion was assigned to battlefield salvage, two more men were killed and four wounded by anti-personnel mines. Millions of landmines were left in the Western Desert after the war, where they still kill or maim the unlucky or unwary.

On 4 November Monty issued a thrilling communiqué:

The enemy has just reached the breaking point and is trying to get his army away. The Royal Air Force is taking a heavy toll of his columns moving west on the main coast road. The enemy is in our power and he is just about to crack. I call on all the troops to keep up the pressure and not relax for one moment. We have the chance of putting the whole Panzer Army in the bag and we will do so.

It was clear that the Eighth Army had the upper hand. For 48 hours there had been a tremendous amount of traffic on the desert tracks and the road, moving west. Major Oswald said we would move soon. Jerry was pulling out, fast.

At 0800 on 7 November we left Alamein for Mersa Matruh. The coast road was a solid stream of vehicles tip to tail. Fighter-bombers roared over to strafe and bomb the Afrika Korps' retreating columns. Rommel's forces had suffered huge material losses and many casualties. We passed several thousand Italian prisoners in a line trudging east, with many more to come, and saw the black, bloated bodies of Germans about the battlefield. There were countless burned-out vehicles, panzers with gun turrets blown off, abandoned artillery, and airstrips littered with wrecked planes. Traffic jams were extraordinary, more than Ascot or Derby Day must ever have been. Where the road was impassable we drove across the desert, after we passed the battlefield's minefields.

It was exhilarating to speed in Desert Formation: the armoured cars scouted several kilometres ahead of the main group, which had a G3 navigator, two tank troops and Monty's 'charger' 400 metres up front; the ACV, the army commander's caravan, staff cars, Bantams and trucks were in the centre; ack-ack was on the flanks and my four trucks were at the rear. Each move we made followed the same routine: Reveille 0600; trucks loaded, breakfast. Order of march: armoured cars, ACV, Ops, ack-ack, Jocks; aircraft spotters on each vehicle, if attacked, trucks stop, disperse, engage with light machine-guns; watch out for mines; vehicles at 100 yard intervals . . . If there was no danger, we would stop for lunch at 1230, move on to recce and set up night camps, then have dinner at 1700 followed by drinks in the mess.

Outside Mersa Matruh we got the vehicles sorted out and personnel settled in. I heard that the town was clear, so went there with Nobby Clark, the ack-ack OC, to see what we could find. Not much: a few prisoners, a few Arabs; a mosque, other buildings looted and damaged and a big Italian ship sunk in the harbour. We were almost the first people there. Some Kiwis warned us of booby traps. I picked up a camp bed, a camera, cigarette lighter and cigars among scattered odds and ends; there was quite a bit of drink too, brandy and liqueurs, and an abandoned truck loaded with Jerry Christmas mail. Further along the coast Sidi Barrani was a pile of rubble. In the desert there were many dust-blown graves, ours and theirs, from the fighting since 1941.

At Tac HQ we heard a radio recording of Churchill praising Alexander and Montgomery for their 'glorious and decisive victory . . . fought almost entirely by men of British blood from home and from the Dominions'. It seemed fitting that the symbol of the Eighth Army was a Crusader's shield and cross. Every member of Tac HQ felt a marvellous esprit de corps. We were playing a part, however small, in a great enterprise, making history. That may not have been the feeling of the ordinary Tommie or Jock but there was undoubtedly a great spirit throughout the army at that time, nurtured by Monty himself and sustained by his success in the field.

Up ahead of us it rained for two days. Wadis became swamps. We passed flooded wreckage, a sea of equipment discarded by the enemy. The Eighth Army's armoured cars and even tanks got stuck or ran out of fuel and failed to cut off Rommel's retreat. It took a further six months for the Allies to clear out the Afrika Korps and the Italians from North Africa. Montgomery has since been criticised for not pursuing Rommel with more speed and vigour, for being too cautious. But the weather was foul and, because the line of supply was stretched and the port of Tobruk destroyed, the Eighth Army ran short of petrol and ammunition—the same problem Rommel had when he raced for the Nile.

Monty's intensive troop training, reinforcements and build up of weaponry had ensured that the Afrika Korps was outnumbered in men, tanks, artillery and aircraft by a factor of about two to one. The Battle of El Alamein did not go entirely according to plan but the Eighth Army had enough reserves to win what turned out to be a slogging match. Monty would have been a spectacularly incompetent general to have lost it. In a message to the troops on 12 November he boasted: 'There are no German and Italian soldiers on Egyptian territory except prisoners. In three weeks we have completely smashed the German and Italian Army, and pushed the fleeing remnants out of Egypt, having advanced ourselves nearly 300 miles.' Most of the PoWs were Italian because the fleeing Afrika Korps abandoned its ally and took its trucks, leaving three of Mussolini's divisions stranded in the desert. The 15th and 21st Panzer divisions escaped, reportedly with less than 50 tanks.

Major Coulson and the RTR chaps left to return to Amiriya because there was now no danger of ground attack. At Sollum the road twisted up

Halfaya 'Hellfire' Pass, an escarpment which jutted out to the sea. I looked back from the summit and saw what seemed like every vehicle in the Eighth Army snaking up from sea level in low gear. We dispersed quickly when a couple of Junkers 88s flew over. The road was bombed several times and some of our trucks were damaged. After crossing the Egyptian/Libyan frontier on 15 November we passed Fort Capuzzo, the first of several Beau Geste-style Italian forts on Via Balbia, the paved two-lane highway from Tripoli. It was a colonial road built for Mussolini's troops and settlers in Cyrenaica, once the breadbasket of the Roman empire. Between Tobruk and Martuba our column came under air attack again. Our officers' mess truck was destroyed and the cook and mess corporal, both good chaps, killed. I saw another unit's Bren carrier and a 3-tonner, within five minutes of each other, blown up on mines. The sight of sudden death and destruction left me strangely unmoved. Similar incidents up ahead held up traffic for hours, which forced the advance party I was with to sleep by the roadside.

On 18 November Tac HQ arrived at Martuba and lingered for ten days. The weather was cold with heavy rain. Airfields had been captured. Monty flew to Cairo to meet with Alexander. We had tremendous parties in the mess, making merry on Italian wine and brandy. Major Oswald in expansive mood told good stories of army life in Egypt and the desert at the beginning of the war. Four of my Jocks went AWOL, desperate for a drink, dirty scoundrels. They returned and were each forfeit a week's pay, a light punishment. I wasn't unsympathetic given the example we officers set.

We moved on to Benghazi, driving across the Jebel, the upland area inland and west from Martuba. The region was surprisingly green with trees and wildflowers, the land misty at dawn and weather spring-like during the day. There were numerous abandoned Italian settlements with white stucco buildings like those in Abyssinia. We by-passed Benghazi before stopping on 1 December. I sent Bloomie in to get Naafi supplies while I visited the field cashier there with Clark. I had seen shocking traffic manners on the road in Cyrenaica and was guilty myself that day. In top gear in my 15-cwt truck I approached an escarpment on the Benghazi road, unaware that it was steep and winding. Unable to change down in time I had a terrifying downhill run, overtaking, braking and lurching all over the road before it levelled out. The town had fallen on 20 November, the fifth time it had changed hands during the war. The Casa Municipal was back in Eighth Army hands and the Banca d'Italia was again the Royal Navy HQ. Empty avenues were lined with the first four-storey buildings I had seen since Alexandria. The harbour was destroyed and there was much bomb damage. Back at camp that evening Clark and I got shamefully drunk on Canadian Club, and I argued with Bloomfield who was in one of his 'gloomy Bloomie' moods. Three more privates went AWOL. One returned alone, followed by the others who had been arrested by the Military Police after beating up two Arabs. I was happy to let Camp Commandant, Captain Adams, deal with them. Inactivity and dull routine, and moving on for more of the same, were sapping morale among the men. I asked Major Oswald if we could be relieved of our duties and let him know we were fed up and longing to get back to our battalion. He said he'd see what he could do.

Monty returned on 10 December. Tac HQ was now 50 kilometres south of Beda Fomm, where Wavell's army had routed the Italians in February 1941. At El Agheila, 130 kilometres further on, Rommel was expected to make a stand. El Agheila had been the limit of Wavell's advance, and of Auchinleck's before the calamitous retreat to El Alamein. Now, the 7th Armoured, 2nd New Zealand and 51st Highland divisions moved up as Monty prepared for another set-piece battle. Faced with the Eighth Army's firepower and a flanking manoeuvre, Rommel lived up to his nickname and vanished into Tripolitania.

Nobby Clark left to rejoin his battery which had been detached at Benghazi. He had been a good companion, yet I never saw him again. All of us at Tac HQ, indeed all who met in the Forces then, understood we had been brought together by chance. We relished our fellowship but few of us sought or expected any permanence in war.

On 18 December I moved off with an advance party for Marble Arch, a colossal art deco folly visible from miles away astride the ribbon of road crossing the Cyrenaica/Tripolitania frontier. The arch had been built to commemorate Mussolini's visit to North Africa in 1937, when he opened Via Balbia. Like his empire, the Latin inscription on the monument was fading. We bivouacked by the roadside, hungry and cold. It was a bleak spot with salt flats all around. Next morning Oswald and I found a new site near the sea for Tac HQ and settled in. An airfield nearby had been cleared of mines and we watched Dakota transport planes land with fuel and stores for the DAF, whose fighter-bombers arrived shortly after. I found a Jerry food dump to which we helped ourselves, careful to check for booby traps. Monty's crew arrived at 1700, along with the rest of my platoon. Brass from Eighth Army HQ dined in the mess that night, their visit accompanied by sporadic ack-ack fire. Oswald said our relief would turn up soon.

Soldiers and tanks streamed through Marble Arch, among them 7th Battalion, the Argylls, on their way up the line. I chatted briefly with some of the officers. One recalled the tremendous bombardment and hearing the skirl of the pipes as he advanced at El Alamein. He said it seemed a long time ago. I was beginning to feel the same about my platoon's bodyguard duties which had lasted for three months. At midday on 24 December our relief platoon turned up. I completed the changeover quickly and asked Monty, through his aide-de-camp, if he would pose for a photograph with my platoon. He accepted. I got Bloomfield to smarten up the men and assemble them in three ranks near the beach. Monty, wearing battledress and his non-regulation two-badge beret, was amiable and gave an edifying talk. He thanked me for the platoon's tour at Tac HQ. Then, hands clasped behind his back and head angled to look each man in the eye, he inspected the platoon. The low sun lit his face and cast long shadows across the sand. I had arranged for Captain Geoffrey Keating of the Army Film and Photo Unit (whose film *Desert Victory* made Montgomery and the Eighth Army famous) to use his camera and mine, so I could get prints for the men.

'The light's going. We'll never get this picture,' he muttered.

I took my place with Monty in the centre of the ranks. Photos taken, he turned to me and declared: 'Good show! See that the pictures are published in the Glasgow papers.' We gave him three cheers and he left. I had a farewell in the Officers' Mess and dished out Christmas beer and Naafi cigarettes to the men.

We drove away from Marble Arch on Christmas Day and arrived at Amiriya at midnight on 31 December. Early on New Year's Day 1943 I got the platoon back to Alex, where we found our battalion at Mustapha barracks. On 23 January the Eighth Army entered Tripoli, three months to the day from the first barrage at El Alamein. Alexander reported to Churchill:

Sir, the orders you gave me on August 10, 1942, have been fulfilled.

His Majesty's enemies, together with their impedimenta, have been completely eliminated from Egypt, Cyrenaica, Libya, and Tripolitania.

I now await your further instructions.

6 The Shores of Sicily

In March 1943 the battalion moved across the Sinai Desert to a tented camp on the Palestine coast 50 kilometres north of Tel Aviv. The Argylls were to form the nucleus of a new Combined Operations formation, 33 Beach Brick, one of several such teams which would land, defend and distribute all the paraphernalia needed to sustain a seaborne invasion of enemy territory. This was a novel assignment for us, training for an imminent invasion of Europe we assumed. Where that would be we were not told and speculation was rife. The team was composed of an infantry battalion (1st Argylls), plus two infantry companies of the Frontier Force Rifles (Indian Army), Royal Artillery ack-ack, Royal Engineers (sappers), RAF and Royal Navy liaison officers, and officers and men from the army's medical, signals, pioneer and transport corps: a total of 125 officers and 2,056 men commanded by our CO, Lieutenant-Colonel McAlister.

In mid-May, on a desert plain near Damascus, we had a dry run simulating landing and setting up positions. The landscape retained its biblical resonance on the drive north along the shores of Lake Galilee. The plain was east of Mount Hermon and at night the wind from its snowy peak, the first snow I had seen since I left the UK in January 1941, was perishing cold. The training was meant to be realistic, so we slept in the open on hard ground, clad only in khaki shirt, shorts and pullovers. I kipped down with our signals officer, Lieutenant Scott-Barrett, who had accompanied me on night patrols on Ruweisat Ridge. He and I unrolled army maps and wrapped them around ourselves trying to keep warm. We saw little of Damascus, going into the city only once, splashing out in a French restaurant and drinks at a cabaret where we were entertained by belly dancers. The Vichy régime had been in control in Syria and Lebanon until 1941 when it was toppled during an Allied campaign from Palestine, which was now militarised with army camps and soldiers everywhere.

I received a telegram from my brother Cecil with the news that in April my father had died. He'd had heart trouble since the blitz on Glasgow two years before. I remember him as a quiet, reserved, God-fearing man and a rather remote figure in my boyhood and youth. I took the news badly, but remember the kindly sympathy I received from my friends Mac and Shaw. Letters from home were a comfort and inspiration all the time I was overseas and I knew I would miss his. He had been a regular correspondent, as my mother was. She was left to cope alone because her four sons were now in the Forces. When I got back to Alex, I arranged for a draft from my pay to be sent to her every month.

At the end of May we moved to a camp near Port Tewfiq. Officers went on courses at Combined Operations at Kabrit or kept the men training. We had a real exercise with 17 Brigade, the RAF and the navy, with warships and landing craft in the Gulf of Aquaba. Then we were confined to camp where Monty visited us and gave a pep talk, a sure sign something was on. The only clue to our destination was that our vehicles' desert camouflage was painted over in olive green. I was promoted Captain and second-in-command of A Company. My new CSM was Jimmy Stewart, the abusive instructor from infantry training at Stirling. He had joined the battalion, became a sergeant and had been promoted. I got the measure of him by reminding him of my recruit days in Balaclava Squad, told him to be sure to treat my men with more respect and consideration than he had done us and added, 'Don't complain, you're the one who told me to apply for a commission.' I had no trouble from him after that.

On 29 June we woke to see five big ships waiting offshore. We spent the day embarking, the Argylls on the *Duchess of Bedford*, a Canadian Pacific liner built in 1928 at Clydebank, requisitioned by the Admiralty in 1939. The duchess looked the worse for wear. I recognised her from the convoy that had taken me to Egypt in 1941. Some of the crew told me they had evacuated refugees from Singapore in January 1942, and landed troops during the British and American invasion in November of French North Africa. Now the ship was loaded with A Company, 1st Argylls, stores and equipment, and over 1,000 men of other units. We stowed our gear and lay on our bunks or hammocks panting in the heat. At sunset on 30 June our convoy formed up slowly in single line ahead to enter the Suez Canal for a night passage. By morning we were anchored with dozens of other ships under a cloud of barrage balloons in the harbour at Port Said. Shore leave was forbidden. We sailed on the morning of 5 July. The kilometre-long breakwater and the statue of Ferdinand de Lesseps, the builder of the Suez Canal, slipped away astern as we cleared the mole in the early light. We were joined by escort destroyers and steamed west. The RAF and the Navy saw to it that we were not molested and, but for the warlike preparations on board and the protective screen of destroyers all round and planes above the convoy, we might have been on a Mediterranean cruise.

Some way into the voyage the battalion was assembled in companies on deck where we stood in silence waiting to be briefed by the CO. The only sounds were the ship's engines and the sea.

'At ease, gentlemen,' he ordered. 'Let me tell you what we've all been waiting for.'

Then we heard his electrifying news.

'We are going to invade Sicily and knock Mussolini out of the war!'

Our convoy was an inspiring sight but paled to insignificance when we met up with other ships. We joined a huge convoy of liners, a cruiser, destroyers and landing craft that was part of an armada which had sailed from Egypt, French North Africa, North America and the Clyde to converge off the south coast of the island. We were in the Eastern Task Force (Eighth Army, Monty); our flank would be secured by a Western Task Force (American Seventh Army, Lieutenant-General George S. Patton).

We approached the shores of Sicily on 9 July. Gale force winds swept the sea. By dusk we were wallowing 60 kilometres off the coast and feeling hellish. To add to our jolly mood every man was given anti-malaria pills because the plain north of the beach was known to be infested by mosquitos. No lights showed on the *Duchess of Bedford* or on any other ships.

In the mess we were given a spoof menu:

Special breakfast for Sicilian tourists: Stewed Fruit of the Island.

Oats, rolled by Commandos. Fresh Fish knocked unconscious by the first LCAs (artillery landing craft); Grilled Breakfast Bacon, Fried Eggs, next issue from Café Royal, Palermo . . . Seven Days' Leave for Milan Cathedral . . . nota bene, do not fail to visit the famous ruins of Syracuse, especially the brand new lot created by that Cultural Society, the RAF. Happy landings. Good luck. Keep your feet dry.

I leafed through my copy of the *Soldier's Guide to Sicily*, an amusing diversion. The cover showed a fist pointing to a silhouette of the island— a symbol of our invasion fleet and the knockout blow we were expected to give the enemy. Inside there was a Monty-style special message from General Eisenhower, the Allies' C-in-C, and the following text:

Sicily has a long and unhappy history that has left it primitive and undeveloped, with many relics of a highly civilised past. Saint's Day feasts with their odd mixture of operatic songs and pantomime are a feature . . . The Sicilian lives on pasta with tomato sauce. Oranges, lemons, almonds are plentiful; Marsala wine is the popular drink . . . Crime is highly organised in all grades of society; 'gangsterism' in the USA had its origins in Sicilian immigration. Morals are superficially very rigid, being based on the Catholic religion and Spanish etiquette of Bourbon times; they are, in fact, of a very low standard, particularly in agricultural areas. The Sicilian is still, however, well known for his extreme jealousy in so far as his womenfolk are concerned, and in a crisis still resorts to the dagger.

Thus we expected a land of opera singers, saints, violent menfolk and gangsters living in a land plentiful with food, wine and ruins of antiquity. We were to see plenty of ruins in Sicily but they were not the historic kind.

The invasion began in the early hours of Saturday 10 July 1943. The storm had eased. We were about 15 kilometres south of Syracuse and about 15 offshore.

'Give 'em Hell lads', somebody shouted amid cheers as we heard our bombers, and Dakotas carrying paratroops or towing troop-carrying gliders, droning overhead. There had been no sleep for any of us aboard the *Duchess of Bedford* that night: there was the noise of the aircraft and naval gunfire aimed at targets on land; there was the period of waiting and suspense. I studied aerial photographs and plans of the beach while waiting for the call to muster the men. They were cooped up inside the bowels of the ship, their faces lit by red blackout lights. The atmosphere was charged with silence, broken by some nervous chatter; then the organised chaos as men and their gear were assembled in some sort of order to be disembarked. It was eerie and hazardous as we stepped down the gangplanks into the landing craft bobbing up and down beside the ship, and set off past the dark, silent shapes of other craft, which were revealed by sudden flashes of naval guns and the gleam of fires ashore. None of us knew what to expect. An opposed landing perhaps, beaches littered with mines and other obstacles. We were apprehensive if not downright scared. In the pre-dawn pallor my LCI (landing craft infantry) bumped the shallows, the landing ramp splashed down and I plunged into four feet of Mediterranean and waded ashore.

I remember first light because we were strafed by two 109s. I saw them climb away glinting in the sun, which promised a clear hot day. The assault troops of 6th Seaforth Highlanders and 2nd Royal Scots Fusiliers had landed successfully on our beach an hour or so before us and mopped up what little enemy opposition there was. They moved inland to Cassibile, a village two kilometres inland where some resistance was overcome, and pushed on to Syracuse, the nearest port and their objective. The only casualties we suffered on landing were Captain Macalister Hall who was wounded by a mine and evacuated, and a soldier killed by the same trap. Eight others Jocks died that first day, buried in their slit trenches by the sand and debris blown up by bomb bursts or hit by shrapnel in the open.

A glance out to sea revealed the epic scale of the invasion. There were hundreds of vessels: warships, troopships, tank and infantry landing craft. At the water's edge beachmasters with semaphore flags directed craft approaching the shore which was soon awash with LCIs and LCTs (tank landing craft), their ramps crashing in the surf. Thousands of soldiers waded and tanks surged through the shallows. Barrage balloons floated above the fleet and a string of them was raised to protect the beach. Ack-ack batteries were dug in. Spitfires from Malta provided initial air cover. To the fighter pilots the beach must have looked like an ant hill. From my point of view it was like an enormous construction site.

By 0830 Beach Brick HQ had been set up in an orchard. Our work was dirty, hot and round-the-clock. The unit's task was to defend the beach (which proved unnecessary), clear mines and mark dispersal trails to get the constant stream of men, tanks, trucks and equipment to camouflaged parking areas, fuel depots or to flow inland. Steel mesh tracks were laid, signs planted and traffic directed. DUWK amphibious vehicles shuttled between the ships and the beaches and onto the roads. We employed Italian prisoners as labour. Despite the air attacks over 11,000 men, 500 vehicles and 90 tons of equipment and stores passed through 'George' beach (as it was coded) in the first 24 hours of the landings, and much more on the beaches where other British and US forces had landed. We knew nothing of them of course, concerned only with the work on hand and with our own safety and survival.

One shocking incident sticks in my mind. Enemy air raids were less frequent after the first day but one caught us on the hop and we rushed for cover. When it was over we found Captain Tidmarsh, our highly respected company commander, hero of Sidi Barrani and Crete, cowering in his slit trench shaking with fear. He had seen more action than most and reached breaking point. He was never the same man again. As second-in-command of the company I found myself burdened with more responsibility as I tried to take some of the weight off his shoulders.

Air cover over the beachhead improved three days into the invasion when the Desert Air Force (which continued as the Eighth Army's close air support) arrived to operate from captured airfields. Kittyhawks and Spitfires flew over, preparing to land on a dusty airstrip bulldozed across a vineyard at Cassibile. We had few opportunities of leaving the beach and never ventured very far inland. MacDougall, Shaw and I visited the debris of Cassibile and the untouched baroque streets of Noto, another liberated town. In both we were given a cautious rather than an ecstatic welcome. We saw evidence of local Fascists having been arrested and mal-treated. The locals may not have had much love for us, but they had even less for Mussolini's henchmen and the Tedeschi, as the Italians called the Germans.

South-east Sicily was taken in three days. Monty arrived with Tac HQ from Malta on 11 July. The port at Syracuse was opened on the 14th. George beach was kept operating and we were kept at work. We saw the 1st Canadian Armoured Brigade's tanks clanking ashore; 78th Division disembarked with 8th Argylls whom we piped ashore; 7th Argylls also landed on Sicily, with the 51st Highland Division. The 51st had been revitalised after Dunkirk where it had been trapped by a German panzer division led by Rommel. Remnants of the 7th and 8th Argylls escaped by sea from Le Harve and the battalions were re-formed.

On 27 July our beach tour ended abruptly when we were moved to the front line. After a hasty clear out the battalion set off in Jeeps, trucks and Bren carriers. Along the coast to the north of us a fierce battle raged near Catania. We skirted that and drove towards Mount Etna. We had orders to join the 1st and 7th Black Watch and 7th Argylls in a 51st Division sector in the Sferro hills south of the volcano. The harsh rocky hill country favoured defence. The German tactics which held us up all through the Italian campaign were simple and effective: defend a line or position, move back to another each time we advanced; make us pay a heavy price in casualties for every village, river and mountain ridge or hilltop.

We trudged along stoney tracks in prickly-pear cactus country. The heat and dust were as uncomfortable as the desert. We were used to that and wore our desert outfit 'khaki drill' shirts and shorts, but we were not used to footslogging. We had trucks in the desert. Since the army in its wisdom had not provided pack animals for hilly Sicily we had to carry everything ourselves. At every rest stop we slumped exhausted in the shade of olive groves, ditches or drystone walls. The rolling countryside, progressively bleak and hilly, was dotted with austere, melancholy villages punctuated by the dome or campanile of a baroque church. Villagers would peek out of doorways and watch us, sometimes with welcoming smiles and gestures. At one bivouac we were befriended by a trio of hungry ragamuffins who approached us cautiously like sparrows, snatched food from our hands and scampered away. But they came back and hung around cadging food and chocolate which we bribed them with to bring us eggs and tomatoes. The deployment with the 51st Division was short. We occupied a ridge on the front line but were not in any attacks, being spectators during the main push one night. By day we crouched baking in our sangars. There was a stream in a shaded wadi below us. When the fighting moved north groups of us took turns to strip off and sprawl in its shallow, pebble pools. Paradise!

We were withdrawn and based for a couple of weeks near Catania which was captured on 5 August. It was off limits but I took the company Jeep and got in with Mac and Shaw. I remember it as the first Italian city I saw, a dour town of black lava stone façades with a baroque cathedral at its core. There had been some civil unrest, with looting, Fascist offices trashed, scores settled. No evidence of the Mafia though. That was in the US Army sector where Italian-American liaison officers were assisted by Mafioso who surfaced as Fascism sank. Mussolini had squashed the Mafia. Expediency and the Yanks brought it back.

If our CO hoped the battalion would play a fighting role with the 51st he was to be disappointed. We were assigned to form a beach brick for the invasion of the Italian mainland. The Jocks didn't mind, nor did I. Life on the beachhead was preferable to risking life and limb in an infantry attack. While we waited there was a round of military parades, film shows and football matches to keep the troops occupied. Some of my Jocks broke open casks of wine in a farmhouse cellar and got hopelessly drunk. Mac, Shaw and I had our first taste of Marsala, which fairly went to our heads. In the circumstances, the food and wine of Sicily tasted like nectar. We took the Jeep as far as we could up Mount Etna and then struggled up a few hundred feet of lava-strewn screes. The reward was a panoramic view of the mountains of Calabria across the Straits of Messina which we were soon to cross. As we drove back we passed several farms. The contadini working the fields took little notice of us unless we asked for help which they gave often. Their stone farmhouses provided shelter for soldiers on both sides and many were destroyed by the fighting. The peasants bore this disruption with fatalism and dignity. Sicily had known many invaders and occupiers. I daresay we were more welcome than some. But I felt, recalling the faded beauty of Noto, that the island would remain the same after we moved on, crumbling in poverty and aristocratic decay. I don't believe we changed much in Sicily, except to add to the ruins that were already there.

After initial setbacks, the campaign came to a speedy end with the rival forces commanded by Patton and Monty racing for Messina (captured by Patton) but failing to trap the enemy. Some 40,000 German and 60,000 Italian troops escaped across the Straits of Messina to Italy with guns and vehicles galore. Suspicion and ill feeling between those two Allied leaders under Alexander's slack control bedevilled operations. The subsequent campaign in Italy was similarly affected, when the American commander Mark Clark's suspicions of the British amounted to paranoia, and Monty's contempt for the Yanks was equally strong and unconcealed. The remoteness of High Command located in Algiers contributed to the Straits of Messina fiasco. On that occasion the Allied air forces were ineffective. The main cause was caution by the Royal Navy, unwilling to risk its ships in narrow waters (or fearful of repeating the attempt to force the Dardanelles in 1915, when battleships were lost to Turkish mines). Whatever the blame the Allies lived to rue the day, as they endured a year and a half hard slog up the length of Italy against resourceful and determined German resistance led by Field Marshal Kesselring. We were to endure that hard slog and face that fanatical resistance, in the mountains north of Florence during the awful winter of 1944–1945.

At 0335 on 3 September 1943, the fourth anniversary of the start of the war, the Straits of Messina exploded with an 'Alamein barrage', a ferocious 600-gun bombardment. The sky sang with shells from Sicily as we chugged across the straits in the dark, watching the barrage straddle the enemy coast. All this turned out to be a complete waste of ammo. When we hit the beach four kilometres north of Reggio di Calabria at 0615 our landing was unopposed. We were slightly dazed by the silence after the profligate bombardment. If someone had bothered to recce the beaches, I thought, or done some aerial reconnaissance, the shelling of an unde-fended coastline should surely have been avoided. But Monty had the firepower and there was an inevitability in its use.

After Sicily our beach brick dealt easily with constant streams of sol-diers and vehicles of the 5th British and 1st Canadian divisions—5,300 vehicles in the first three days. Monty landed on the first morning, no doubt to see the results of his bombardment. The Germans chose not to defend Calabria, preferring to regroup further north on the Gustav Line. We saw no Jerries but we bagged Italians, hundreds of the blighters, whose white flags had been waved the moment we landed. Some Jerry planes evaded our fighters and strafed and bombed the beaches, killing one of our men and wounding five.

On 8 September we heard that Italy had surrendered. Mussolini, deposed by his own government after the Sicily landings, was spirited north by the Germans to form a puppet régime which continued the war. On 9 September the Allies landed at Salerno; Taranto was taken after a seaborne landing. 'Rome by Christmas', the generals said. We were relieved of our beach duties and spent a month on the Calabrian coast reorganising and retraining. I recall the fate of my company commander, Captain Tidmarsh. He had gone out one evening with the CSM and another warrant officer on the prowl looking for wine and women. They ended up at a farmhouse where they were attacked by the outraged father protecting his daughter. Our captain received blow to the head and was flown home for treatment. He had just been decorated, an MC for his ser-vice in the Middle East. As second-in-command I took temporary charge of A Company. I never saw him again.

The battalion moved by road and rail to Taranto where we were not surprised to be ordered to the docks. Throughout the war the battalion's postings and tasks were unpredictable and often unconventional. We thought we might join the 51st Highland Division which was return-ing to the UK to train for the D-Day landings in Normandy. Instead we sailed back to Egypt where we were posted to Mena camp outside Cairo, for security duty at the Mena House Conference. The conference was attended by Churchill, Roosevelt, Chiang Kai-Shek, a Russian delegation, Alan Brooke and other top brass, aides-de-camp, politicians, interpreters, reporters and cameramen. The setting was Mena House Hotel, built as a royal lodge for Khedive Ismail in the shadow of the Great Pyramid. The Jocks wore kilts and performed their ceremonial Changing of the Guard with a special swagger to impress the Ruskies, Chinese and Yanks. One of our officers, Captain Jim Sceales, was assigned ADC to Chiang Kai-Shek. Officers were given passes to eat at the hotel and use its amenities. I had the unusual experience of finding myself standing next to Lord Louis Mountbatten at the urinals in the gents' lavatory.

'Fine fellows, your chaps,' he said.

'Yes, indeed, sir. Thank you, sir.' I agreed, surprised that I found my voice and that he had bothered to speak to me. He was a popular figure, formerly the captain of the destroyer HMS *Kelly* when it was bombed and sunk off Crete.

I had an even more surprising encounter when we returned to Alex. I met my brother Cecil, commissioned at an OCTU in Devon as a second lieutenant in 42 Royal Marine Commando. He'd sailed from the Clyde in November en route to India. His ship was bombed in the Med and in port for repairs. He phoned around various camps on the off chance of finding the Argylls. When I saw he'd been promoted he laughed and said that his CO, thinking it a slur on the Royal Marines for one of his officers to have a younger brother a captain in the Argylls, had made him a full lieutenant. Mac, Shaw and I took him and a fellow marine officer, David Hardy, and some Forces girls we knew for drinks at the Cecil Hotel and a Christmas dinner at the Union Club. That evening we sang and strolled along the Corniche without a care in the world. A few days later Cecil and Hardy rejoined their ship and sailed for Bombay. Cecil never said much about his war. He played cricket and sent me photos which always showed him in the company of attractive girls, evidently taken at some palm-fringed beauty spot or hill station. He joked that the only time he was wounded was in India, when he fell off a motorbike. But I do know that 42 Royal

Marine Commando trained for combined operations and jungle warfare in 1944. Cecil went into action against the Japanese, in the mangrove swamps, paddy fields and jungle of the Arakan on the coast of Burma in January 1945.

Argylls with long service overseas were repatriated at the end of 1943. Those of us who stayed moved to a desert camp near Suez to train replacements. It was there that I met a friend from home, Willie Rankine, a private in 2nd Battalion, the Cameron Highlanders. Our meeting was brief, as I was about move off and his battalion had just arrived to take over the camp. Cecil and I were in the same cricket team as Willie and his brother Davie before the war. I'd met Davie, a private in the Royal Army Service Corps, in Cairo some time before (he died of typhus in Egypt in 1943). Willie fought in Italy but we didn't see each other again until after the war. Given the confusion and mass movement of troops during the war years those coincidental meetings still amaze me.

At the end of January the battalion entrained for Port Said for immediate embarkation on HMT *Dilwara*, which had been in our convoy to Sicily. The ship was modern, built specifically as a troopship. The CO and a new padre, Rev. Dow, conducted a service on deck to commemorate the 150th Anniversary of the Raising of the Regiment. Kipling's 'Recessional' and the 91st Psalm drifted across the Med as we stood in silence and prayer. It was 1100 hours, 6 February 1944. Two days later we entered the lagoon at Taranto harbour to join the Italian campaign.

7 The Gustav Line

We disembarked at Taranto, an Italian naval base battered by the war. The waterfront was lined with a castello and ochre-coloured palazzi, some damaged by bombs. It was in one of those grandiose hulks that the ever truculent MacDougall got us mixed up in a bar room brawl. He and I were with some South African and Rhodesian officers who had just joined the battalion, drinking in a hastily-established officers' club. It was more like a wild west saloon and, sure enough, a scrap started. Mac was outraged at the noisy behaviour of a group of junior officers fresh off the boat from Blighty. In particular, he was offended at the way one of them was wearing his kilt. Hanging too low over his knees, Mac said. He moseyed over and a heated argument ensued. Things looked to be turning nasty so I went across to try to cool him off. One of the new arrivals laid a hand on my shoulder and tried to pull me away.

'Take your hand off me!' I shouted, twice, and when he refused floored him. His pals piled in. At that moment, two senior officers appeared.

'What the bloody hell's going on?'

We were separated quickly and peace was restored. Mac and the 'Zulus' (as we called the South Africans and Rhodesians) loved it. After that roughhouse I became known as a 'hard man', a reputation that did me no damage.

The battalion spent three weeks under canvas at a staging area outside Taranto, training and re-equipping for combat. We were kitted out with battledress, leather jerkins, winter boots, gloves, scarves, balaclavas and gas capes. Bren carriers were taken over from another regiment; Jeeps, 15-cwt trucks and 3-ton lorries from Egypt were picked up at the docks. Our CO, Lieutenant-Colonel McAlister, visited Eighth Army HQ at Vasto on the Adriatic coast and toured the 8th Indian Division's front line. A move was imminent, to join the division's 19 Brigade.

At 0500 on 25 February 1944 we left Taranto in convoy with full tanks of petrol and 100 miles reserve for a 300-kilometre drive up the coast. I was with the advance party (the CO, the adjutant, company commanders and other officers), followed at intervals by the main vehicle party (subalterns, NCOs and men), and a rail party (tracked vehicles, mortars and 6-pounder A/T guns and all their crews). I rode with my new company commander, Major Lossock, a veteran of Sidi Barrani. We passed Vasto that afternoon. At the river Sangro near our destination we crossed a Bailey bridge, its portable steel trusses bolted together to form an impressive long span. The original bridge had been destroyed by Allied bombing or by the retreating Germans. We overtook dozens of mules led by Indian soldiers, plodding in single-file columns on unpaved roads. Red Cross tents, bivouacs, tanks and trucks were scattered along wide shallow valleys. At every hamlet troops clustered around braziers and steaming cookhouses, drinking tea and stamping their feet to keep warm.

Our new sector was a rumpled landscape below the Abruzzi mountains, whose peaks were ominous and capped with snow. A blizzard on Hogmanay had left 3-metre deep drifts across the Gustav Line which zig-zagged from the Adriatic to the Tyrrhenian Sea. 'Sunny Italy', Lossock observed. Churchill called it 'the soft underbelly of Europe' hoping it would provide a swift route to Berlin. That was optimistic.

The CO stopped at Lanciano, a medieval hill town where Divisional HQ had been set up. We were billeted in another town, Castelfrentano, and in nearby stone-walled farmhouses with earth floors and open-hearth fires. Conditions in the countryside were primitive, but since the contadini put up with these living conditions and were friendly I thought it churlish to complain. Throughout the Italian campaign we were surprised by the kindness of the poorest people, hardy peasants who worked the land in return for basic accommodation and half the fruit of their labour (the other half went to the landowner at harvest time). The Germans stole their pigs and cattle. We were grateful for the straw that had been left because we slept in the empty byres. We fortified ourselves with a nightly ration of rum and kept fires roaring day and night, mindful of a Brigade

HQ order not to cut down olive trees or telegraph poles.

The CO, Major MacFie and I toured the Sangro battlefield which was strewn with rusting debris from Monty's November offensive. The land was waterlogged and shell-holed. Burned-out tanks lay slumped like drunks by the roadside. The front was now static following a big push in December which had stalled in atrocious weather. At the end of 1943 Monty had been recalled to the UK, where he was promoted to command the British and Canadian armies preparing for D-Day. On New Year's Day 1944 he issued a final message to the army he had made famous:

You have made this Army what it is; you have made its name a household word all over the world; you must uphold its good name and its traditions. And I would ask you to give to my successor the same loyal and devoted service that you have never failed to give to me.

His understudy, Lieutenant-General Leese, took over—the same gung ho Leese who had stood with Bloomie and me as we watched the Alamein barrage. For Leese promotion couldn't have come at a worse time. The Eighth Army was stuck in mid-winter on the Gustav Line. The 8th Indian Division's three brigades (17th, 19th and 21st) were scattered across the front; 1st Argylls had been moved up to relieve 19 Brigade's 1/5th Essex Regiment which had lost almost 100 men in the recent fighting. The brigade's other infantry units were 6th Battalion, 13th Frontier Force Rifles and 3rd Battalion, 8th Punjab Regiment. Artillery support was provided by the 53rd Field Regiment (25-pounders) and infantry support by the 14th Canadian Armoured Regiment (Sherman tanks).

The 8th Indian's senior officers were British, as were those who led its brigades, regiments and battalions. I never met an Indian officer above the rank of major. Altogether something of a relic from the Raj, I thought, like the division's CO. He was Major General 'Pasha' Dudley Russell, nicknamed Pasha because of his bushy black moustache, swagger stick and confident manner. He was a Kiplingesque professional soldier, a type now extinct. During the First Word War he was wounded in France and won an MC with Allenby in Palestine. He was on the North-west Frontier between the wars and served with the 5th Indian Division in Eritrea and

Abyssinia, where he negotiated the Duke of Aosta's surrender. He had also been in the Western Desert and won our affection by wearing desert army shorts, except in the coldest weather. Our brigade CO was Brigadier Dobree, 'The Wee Briggie,' also a desert army officer, and a subaltern in the Royal Artillery during the First World War. The Indian Army recruited mainly from the tribal lands of northern India, Nepal and what is now Pakistan. The similarity of the 6/13th Frontier Force Rifles and the 3/8th Punjabis to the traditional composition of Scottish Highland regiments was striking. All the men were volunteers. Their code of personal honour was rooted in tribal, village and family pride. The politics of Indian nationalism, which caused unrest in their homeland during the war, did not affect their conduct or courage, despite propaganda leaflets inciting mutiny which the Germans lobbed over our lines.

Farmhouses in our sector's forward areas were in full view of the enemy, so movement during the day was restricted. A curfew was in place from 1900 and a blackout enforced strictly. The buildings kept out the bitter cold but not enemy shellfire. Fortunately a policy of 'live and let live' was observed during the winter: if we didn't shell Jerry-held houses, Jerry wouldn't shell ours, but other positions were attacked freely and nightly patrols were made in no-man's-land. Troops stuck in sangars and trenches endured the most discomfort. Conditions were pretty awful too for the Italian guides and Indian muleteers of the pioneer platoons who made nightly treks on muddy tracks to bring up supplies to the forward positions where they were often harassed by small-arms and shellfire. It still amazes me that while we were fighting a twentieth-century war, mules were our lifeline in rough country throughout the Italian campaign.

On 8 March we prepared to relieve 17 Brigade's 1st Royal Fusiliers in positions near the villages of Poggiofiorito and Arielli. It was cold and the sky overcast when the battalion set off at 1000 hours, companies at 20-minute intervals on the eight-kilometre approach march across ridges and plateaus 200 to 400 metres in elevation. We were burdened with full kit, and gas capes for the rain which poured all day. At the assembly area near Poggiofiorito, we were fortified by a hot meal and a tot of rum.

Companies moved off before dark to their positions in and around scattered farm buildings much knocked about by shellfire on a low ridge near Arielli. These were hardly a line, more a series of strongpoints facing a similar one on the German side. The relief was completed by 2245.

I was left behind at Poggiofiorito to bring up rations, water, ammo and other stores by mule train. This task was accomplished in pitch darkness, lit occasionally by star shells and tracer fire. Progress was punctuated by the rattle of Jerrycans and ammo boxes carried by the mules and the curses of the muleteers, on muddy tracks full of potholes, the animals stuck frequently or in danger of slipping and falling. Company HQ was a scene of confusion. The takeover from the Fusiliers had not gone smoothly and nobody seemed to know exactly where they were or what they were doing. To make matters worse the Fusiliers had left mines and booby traps scattered about their company position. We started unloading the mules, which refused to stand still. I grabbed one by the leash. It snorted and shied away . . . A sudden flash and an almighty bang and I was blown back, and lay semi-conscious in the mud feeling as if the mule had kicked me. It had stepped on a booby-trapped grenade, taken the full force of the blast and lay whimpering and dying in a heap of boxes. Anything within 20 yards of a grenade exploding will be hit and I was closer than that. 'What a pathetic way to go' went through my mind as I shivered in shock. I'd been hit in the legs by shrapnel.

Voices came near. Lieutenant Bill Dunn, one of my platoon commanders, appeared out of the night and peered at me closely. After establishing that I would live he helped me stagger through the blanketed entrance of Company HQ where I collapsed at the feet of my horrified company commander. It was a bad start to the night's operation for him. A worse one for me. Two Jocks had also been wounded. The other casualties were three bottles of whisky I had brought up for Lossock and his subalterns.

'Sorry we can't give you a dram,' Dunn said. I raised myself on my elbow and stared at him. He nodded. 'All gone. Blown to buggery.'

The ever-resourceful Sanders produced some field dressings and patched me up as best he could. Lossock called for stretcher bearers. I had seen men hit before but didn't know, until that moment, adrenaline can shoot through the system like a drug. I was also numb from the cold as we set off down the hillside. Dunn, who had been with the battalion since Alamein, shouted after me, 'Ray, you owe me a dram.'

Two Indian bearers carried me on the stretcher; the two Jocks were walking wounded. Somehow the bearers negotiated the muddy track in the dark and got me to the casualty clearing station at Battalion HQ where I was dumped on a wooden trestle. A medic gave me a shot of morphine and cleaned and bandaged my wounds. Ronnie McAlister, our experienced, well-respected CO, looked down at me with sad eyes full of sympathy. He was a fine, gentlemanly, kind-hearted man with whom I had got on well in the desert. Perhaps he was not ruthless enough for the job, for he was soon to be replaced. I was mad at the Fusiliers for not clearing their booby traps. But I was glad to be out of the line and away from the hateful hills of Poggiofiorito.

An ambulance took me to an Indian Army field hospital where I was operated upon a couple of days later. Bits of shrapnel were removed (one piece was missed and had to be extracted at Erskine Hospital near Glasgow ten years after the war). After the surgeon operated he asked me if there was anything I would like. I replied, 'Yes, a whisky please.' He laughed and told a nurse to let me have it. Waking up the next morning I heard voices of children at play outside. Having been so long accustomed to the company of soldiers and the noise of battle the happy sound fell on my ears with such moving novelty and clarity that I almost wept. I imagined the shock my mother would get on the doorstep when she received the dreaded War Office telegram: 'I regret to have to inform you . . .' At least it told her I was alive.

My recuperation was at a British army hospital at Barletta on the coast. I felt a bit of a fraud, having minor wounds dressed daily by attentive nurses. Especially as in the next bed to mine there was a young RAF fellow who had severe burns to his hands and face from a plane crash. He groaned and cried out when he had his wounds dressed twice daily. I wrote letters home for him to his dictation in which, bravely, he made light of his condition. He must have been scarred for life.

At the end of May I was ordered to report to the Infantry Base Depot at Benevento 50 kilometres north-east of Naples. The Americans had bombed the place months before. The façade of the eleventh-century cathedral stood like a stage set, the rest of the building having collapsed. In the surrounding countryside gangs of Neapolitans foraged for food. Naples had been liberated at the beginning of October 1943, after the Allies broke out of the Salerno bridgehead and headed for Rome.

I visited Naples. Once was enough. Arriving at Stazione Centrale, I saw a peasant child trip on the platform and fall under a moving train. The boy was sliced in two. The hysterical mother turned and leapt at me, as if I was to blame for the boy's death, for the air raids, the war. Two Carabinieri pulled her away and I escaped, shocked. Outside the station, Piazza Garibaldi was a sea of hustlers, many of them ragged urchins like the boy under the train. The mother had probably brought him in from the country to join this crowd. Now she had lost her bread winner. I was pawed at by aggressive beggars: 'Inglese, Americano, Canadese, Scozzese?' they yelled. It was as if every rat had emerged from the sewers, sniffing the cigarettes and chocolate that the victorious Allied soldiers brought. Naples had been off-limits because of air raids, anarchy and disease since it had fallen to the Allies. Now there were plenty of off-duty soldiers milling around. I found an army club in the bomb-damaged salons of the Royal Palace and had a stiff drink at the bar.

In the Galleria Umberto, a bomb-damaged iron and glass roofed arcade, soldiers strode by arm-in-arm with garish tarts. The place was a black market and everything was for sale, including army stuff stolen by the recently liberated citizens. I suspect some of our rear echelon people and military police indulged the illicit activity, participated in it or simply couldn't stop it. Outside the galleria I found myself in front of San Carlo opera house which had uniformed flunkeys at the door. That evening I sat surrounded by gilded stucco in its auditorium, with an audience of Allied officers and the city's melancholy bourgeoisie seeking refuge and consolation in Puccini and Mozart. Perhaps Naples had always been the city of baroque squalor I saw: poverty and Puccini, the sparkling bay and the Grand Tour beauty of the setting. Mount Vesuvius smouldered in the background, having erupted spectacularly in March. The superstitious Neopolitans were not alone in seeing that as a sign of divine displeasure.

While I had been at Barletta and Benevento IBD the war in Italy had entered a new phase. The Argylls completed an unpleasant tour at Poggiofiorito before being relieved by the 4/16th Punjabis in April. Later that month the 8th Indian Division was trucked across the Abruzzi to the Cassino front. The Argylls began intensive training with the 6/13th Frontier Force Rifles and the 14th Canadian Tank Regiment to take part in a big push to capture Monte Cassino, which blocked the way to Rome.

Route 6 from Naples enters the Liri valley below Monte Cassino where an enormous Benedictine monastery sprawls on the summit, from where German artillery observers brought down shellfire on anything moving on the highway. In January 1944 American and British troops had landed at Anzio to turn the Cassino flank but were contained on the beachhead. Previous attempts to take Monte Cassino had failed. The final battle began at 2300 on 11 May with a massive artillery barrage. The monastery was bombed by American planes and captured by infantry. Polish troops finished the job. The Argylls' part in the great assault had been to cross the river Rapido at the entrance to the valley and secure a bridgehead for 19 Brigade's tanks to pass through. There was confusion in the darkness of the approach march, lumbered as the Jocks were with assault boats, and white tape lines marking the route had been blown away by shellfire. The crossing itself was a nightmare with many boats holed or swept away in the fierce current. Cassino cost the Argylls two officers and 19 other ranks killed and three officers and 76 other ranks wounded.

Among the wounded was my informant Bill Dunn, who had last seen me flat on my back on the Gustav Line. I found him by chance in a hospital at Benevento. His war was over, because he had stepped on a Schu mine. I remember him complaining about the pain in his foot, which wasn't there, and managed to smuggle in a bottle of whisky for him.

'Ray, you remembered.'

I grinned, sharing the irony of the situation.

My posting back to the battalion came through in the last week of June. The day before I left, MacDougall, now promoted to captain but no longer with the battalion, turned up at the depot. He had been detached after the Cassino battle. He told me of his nemesis, our new CO, Lieutenant-Colonel 'Freddie' Graham. Mac was aggrieved and disgruntled and had a disturbing tale to tell. In one of the delaying actions the Germans were so good at he and his men in D Company were pinned down by a Jerry tank in open country with little cover. With only small arms and no artillery or tanks in support there was little he could do but keep his head down. Any movement attracted enemy fire, so he and his men continued to lie low. The delay held up the advance of other units in the battalion and brigade, and the CO got stick from the brigadier. When Graham, at some risk to himself, went forward to investigate he took it out on Mac. Told him he shouldn't have allowed himself to be pinned down, that he should have shown more spirit and dash. Harsh words were exchanged.

'Were you on strike?' Graham asked.

Mac shouted back. 'No, sir. I was waiting for a bus!'

The CO sacked him on the spot. My sympathies were with Mac. It's easy, safe back at Battalion HQ, to criticise those at the sharp end. I helped him to drown his sorrows that night. It would be some time before I saw him again.

The next day I was off on my long awaited return to the battalion. Had I not got the order, I think I'd have cut loose and hitchhiked. The fear of many of us in transit at the IBD was that we could be sent wherever the army's pen-pushers decided. On 4 July 1944, the day that Rome was liberated, I boarded a train for Spoleto with another officer and a draft of 45 new men. Our train steamed along a repaired track into Umbria. We were packed into cattle wagons, so I saw little of the passing and increasingly hilly landscape. Images flitted by like a slide show: Narni picturesque, unspoiled; Terni bombed by Allied planes; Spoleto, the station devastated when a German ammo train had exploded. I found the Argylls camped in olive groves on the slopes below the old town which had been spared.

The battalion had just returned from Assisi which it liberated on 17 June. The Germans had retreated but only after loosing off some spandau fire at the approaching Jocks. To the din of church bells, and there are many churches in the town of St Francis, the Argylls and their vehicles were engulfed by crowds cheering 'Viva i Scozzesi'. During this emotional civic outburst C Company, which had been first into the town, reached Porta San Francesco below the bulwarks of the Basilica. A Jerry mortar stonk landed killing one Jock and wounding three. As the CO wrote later of such incidents: 'Ninety-nine times out of a hundred, they would not have been hit; then the hundredth bomb arrived.' Some unlucky civilians were also killed as they scattered for cover. The Argylls mopped up the area but Jerry, as usual, escaped to the north.

I had a reunion with Shaw and Sanders but not, alas, Bloomfield who had received a home posting after long service overseas (he returned to active service and was wounded in Normandy). Shaw had been promoted captain. He introduced me to a new officer, Lieutenant Stephen White, posted from the 'Kosbies', the King's Own Scottish Borderers. I didn't get back to A Company then but to D Company, as second-in-command to Major Scheurmier (the IO who had sent me the urgent message at Venticinque). I made sure Sanders came with me.

Since hearing Mac's tale of woe I was not looking forward to meeting Lieutenant-Colonel Graham, a tall, black-moustached figure who strode around with a deer-stalking stick. But he turned out to be an admirable CO, a 'soldiers' soldier' who gained the respect and affection of all officers and men. He was born in Helensburgh, my father's home town. We got on well from the start. He had joined the army after Eton in 1927, trained at Sandhurst and served with the Argylls' 2nd Battalion in the Far East and on the North-west Frontier, and with 1st Battalion in Palestine before the war. He was with a Commando brigade on Crete, where he narrowly escaped capture, and had been at Tobruk during the last weeks of the siege. He told me he'd lately been stuck at a desk job in India, then jumped at the chance to get back to the Argylls.

We had another new arrival, a precocious 12 year-old Italian boy who hung around Battalion HQ. It was not unusual to find Italians in our camps (some worked for us), and children on the scrounge for food. What intrigued me was that this boy wore a balmoral and always saluted me smartly. It turned out that Luigi Miniotti, 'Wee Toni', was an orphan who had been adopted by the Jocks. A Jerry shell had destroyed his home and killed his family. One of our cooks, Private Leitch, had found him sleeping in a ditch and fed him. When the battalion moved on Wee Toni followed. Leitch kitted him out and showed him how to salute. Freddie Graham said the boy should be sent to the Red Cross but Mrs Leitch in Glasgow had agreed to foster him, so he stayed. I think we all understood the redemption our new recruit offered us.

At dawn on 8 July we received a 'move at once' order to support the 6th Armoured Division which was stuck on the road to Arezzo. The brigade was advancing up Via Flaminia, that most beautiful of Italian roads, the Roman route of pilgrims and legionaries. We crossed the Tiber and passed below the hill town of Perugia. Lake Trasimeno shimmered in the distance, and vanished in a thunderstorm. Rain slowed the advance and allowed the Germans to regroup. We took over from 7th Battalion, the Rifle Brigade, on a hill north of Cortona, a position which could only be reached on foot. Our job was to neutralise enemy artillery OPs (observation posts) from where shelling was being directed at 6th Armoured's tanks on the main road. One of our platoons stalked a Jerry OP and captured the spotters and their radios. Lieutenant White's platoon lost one Jock killed and another wounded. It was a short but typical deployment. The 6th Armoured was able to press on. A Kiwi battalion took our place and we returned to Spoleto. Jerry was in full retreat.

This was a period of constant movement, mostly in brilliant summer weather. We had long since discarded our battledress, scarves and leather jerkins for more comfortable and familiar khaki shorts and shirts. We criss-crossed Umbria and travelled through Tuscany, being trucked but often marching to new assembly areas to relieve or support other Allied units. At rest stops we foraged for food in fields and farms, as soldiers have done through the centuries. Contadini who had been caught up in the war had little left to barter. Outside a village destroyed by bombing, probably from Allied planes, I found a priest and his flock cowering in a cave. Some were dead, the rest were starving. Concerned about typhus I made my men stand back but gave the priest what food we could spare. Those refugees in the cave still return to haunt me, like a Goya etching from *The Disasters of War*.

One march, to some assembly area or other, was in blistering heat but through pleasant country and on quieter roads. I got off to a bad start, missed a turning and, after marching for about a kilometre, saw no one in front of me. Amid some disgusted rumblings from the ranks I checked my map and about-turned. I spotted a track that seemed to offer a short cut to the right road. As we were resting for a 10-minute break by the roadside, who should appear but Major MacFie, second-in-command, at the head of the battalion. The other companies passed amid jeers and catcalls from my Jocks. Later, the men were smothered in dust raised by passing trucks and tanks. Some of them, against orders, drank too freely from their water bottles, which soon became empty, and they were parched with thirst. There were many stragglers and some with sore feet and heat exhaustion fell out by the wayside. As my luck would have it Pasha Russell passed us. His Jeep slid to a halt. When the dust cleared I saw him looking back, appalled. He gave Wee Briggie a roasting. This was passed on with increasing severity all down the line: to our CO, company commanders and finally to me and my long-suffering Jocks.

We were not the only battalion on the move. Several thousand vehicles were needed to transport an army division and they were often funnelled onto the same route. Bridges had been destroyed, either by our own air forces or blown by Jerry. These demolitions were sometimes covered by small but skilful enemy rearguards. When the traffic did move, the landscape was animated by plumes of dust thrown up by trucks and tanks or shellfire from both sides. Dust trails on the white gravel roads were spotted easily. Signs by the roadside warned 'Danger, no traffic in daytime beyond this point . . . Road under shellfire', and we would be held up until Jerry artillery could be dealt with by tanks or fighter-bombers.

While at Spoleto, Shaw and I managed a day trip to Rome. Like every city we saw overseas it was a novelty because few of us had been abroad before the war. We visited the Colosseum, the Forum and St. Peter's. I knew too little to get the full value from seeing them, unlike the battalion's IO, George Rome, suitably named, who had been an architecture student at Cambridge before the war and was with us that day. In any case we were too involved in the making of modern history to appreciate antiquity. Death and destruction stalked the length and breadth of Italy, mocking the venerated ruins of the past.

I am not the only Eighth Army soldier who felt that the enemy should have been beaten on the road to Rome. But the chance to trap the German Tenth and Fourteenth armies was squandered by Lieutenant-General Mark Clark, the US Fifth Army commander. He had agreed to Alexander's plan that the Americans cut off the German retreat from Cassino, but his war was as much a contest with the British as it was with the Germans. Instead of cutting Route 6 he rushed for Rome, allowing the enemy forces to escape. Clark should have been sacked but he and his entourage, which included a 50-strong public relations team, ensured that on 5 June 1944 he was photographed in his Jeep as the conqueror of the Eternal City He held a press conference and declared: 'It's a great day for the Fifth Army.' He didn't mention the Eighth. Clark's fame and folly were eclipsed by the Allied invasion of Normandy the next day. I remember hearing a BBC radio news bulletin: 'D-Day has come. Early this morning, the Allies began their assault on Hitler's European fortress.' Evidently it was forgotten that we had started that assault the year before. We found ourselves mocked as 'D-Day dodgers', the result of an impudent remark in Parliament. That insult was adopted by Eighth Army soldiers, as a sardonic verse sung to the tune of 'Lili Marlene'. The war in Italy became a strategic sideshow, except for the men on both sides who fought there.

8 Tuscany

Assisi, Arezzo, Perugia, Siena, Florence: the mere recital of these place names takes me back to that summer of 1944 when we pursued the Germans to the river Arno. As Freddie Graham wrote in the battalion history: 'Kesselring's Nazi supermen were in retreat . . . the hunt was up.' On reaching the banks of the river, 'the 91st had won the race!' Our battalion was the first Eighth Army unit to reach the Arno, at Empoli.

We had moved to Siena early on 18 July, en route to an assembly area behind the front line in Val d'Elsa where we took over positions from the Free French. Company transport was the CO's Jeep, one Bren carrier and several 15-cwt trucks. As usual, radio silence was maintained and the vehicles' unit signs concealed, and floors sandbagged as protection against landmines. We were reminded to deploy camouflage nets at rest stops because enemy artillery and air activity was predicted. We saw no Jerry planes—the Allies had complete air superiority. But wars are won or lost on the ground. The Germans still had a formidable army and they managed to move their tanks, troops and artillery around.

The hilltop domes and campanili of Siena glowed in late afternoon sunlight when I arrived after a long drive. Diversions disorganised our staggered convoy and it took until midnight for the battalion to straggle in, to a bivouac near the railway station below the city walls. The station had been bombed but its clock tower was standing with the timepiece stopped, a fitting comment on Mussolini's régime and his boast that he made the trains run on time. Siena was a staging post for the Allied advance. Thousands of soldiers and vehicles were passing through or around it. Generals Alexander, Leese, Clark and Juin (the French commander) had attended a service at the Duomo and a tattoo in Piazza del Campo to mark Bastille Day and the city's liberation by the 3rd Algerian Infantry Division. An American liaison officer with our brigade, Major

John H. Stutesman, wrote of Siena when we corresponded long after the war: 'I remember the languorous summer heat of 1944 when you relieved the French north of Siena. My 88th Infantry Division went into the line south of Volterra, after a brief respite following our assault on Rome, and I was sent off to liaise with our right flank, the French. I entered Siena with their forward elements, no opposition. I was stunned to find the Sienese taking their evening strolls around the town square as though nothing had happened in 400 years, which may be how they felt about us foreigners fighting in Italy.'

We left the city on 20 July for the assembly area. Our task was to clear German positions from high ground between Empoli and Florence. It was on a two brigade front: 19 Brigade in the river Elsa valley; 21 Brigade in Val di Pesa east of us. The CO and company commanders went ahead in the Jeeps to recce the new sector and find the Free French unit we were to relieve. The Bren carriers, trucks, company cookhouses and a mobile bath unit followed later. Most of us marched, led by Major MacFie, with companies following at intervals. Mine, D Company, the HQ company, brought up the rear. Every few kilometres, we passed ruined villages, the calling cards left by the armies of both sides. Places that had existed peacefully for centuries had been abruptly visited by death and destruction, which had then departed as rapidly as they had arrived. Towns previously familiar only to locals and art history cognoscenti appeared with sudden brevity on army communiqués and newspaper headlines. Poggibonsi had the misfortune to be a rail and road junction and was a scene of utter desolation after American bombing. San Gimignano's cluster of medieval towers which were suspected Jerry OPs had been shelled by French artillery. Each side blamed the other for the damage.

After the war I read that the Germans claimed that they tried to prevent Italy's historic sites becoming battlefields. Rome, Assisi, Orvieto, Siena and others were indeed spared by timely evacuation. But the enemy's concern to save Italy's heritage was no less expedient than ours. The French gunners at San Gimignano followed the Allied commanders' stated policy towards Italy's historic monuments: they weren't worth the death of a single Allied soldier. Apparently we employed 'Monuments, Fine Arts and Archives' officers armed with prewar Baedeker guides and lists of monuments to be protected. They operated at battalion and company levels and worked with Italian experts. There was only a handful of them in Tuscany at the time. A list of protected monuments was circulated. I never saw it and I never met a single MFAA officer.

We marched along Val d'Elsa towards Castelfiorentino, 50 kilometres north of Siena but more than that on the route we took. We passed the hill town of Certaldo which rose on our right like a fresco, cracked here and there by French artillery. The valley was cratered by shells and bombs on the approach to Castelfiorentino. We didn't know if the French held it or which parts. Brigade orders were to relieve the 2nd and 4th Moroccan divisions of the French Expeditionary Corps, which had fought through the hills west of Siena, often leading the US Fifth Army's advance. They were being withdrawn, along with an American corps, for an invasion of the south of France. The 'Goums', as the Moroccans were called, were French-officered mountain tribesmen. They wore baggy gaitered trousers and turbans. Some were mounted on tough little ponies. The CO found them just south of the town. Their French officers sporting stylish uniforms and kepis reminded me of the haughty Italians we had captured in Abyssinia, and confirmed my antipathy towards La Gloire. There was a language problem. The situation was not helped by the fact that their HQ people didn't have a clue where their forward troops were. Nor did they seem to be expecting us.

The relief was a fiasco. We completed it and sized up the ground, a two-kilometre-wide valley with low hills on both sides and Castelfiorentino on a hill in front of us. A Company crossed the railway line and the river Elsa to hold the flat ground on the river's west bank. C Company went into the hills to the east. Major Elder's B Company, led into the town by French guides, was shelled by Jerry and forced to hole up under fire for the rest of the day. The next morning D Company went into the line, supported by the 14th Canadian's tanks. We rode in on the them, dismounted and made contact with Elder's beleaguered Jocks. Jerry pulled out of the town. A and

C companies covered our flanks as we pushed forward along the main road to Empoli. Sappers filled in a 'blow' in the road to let the tanks cross. Jerry shelled us off and on all day. Two Jocks were wounded in an ambush, when grenades were thrown by some Jerries hiding in a house. We flushed them out and shot the lot. Their bodies were searched for orders, letters or diaries to be passed to the IO, Captain Rome. Next day Elder's men captured an OP manned by Panzer Grenadiers but the shelling continued. Three Jocks were killed and three wounded. Company HQ was set up in a villa beyond the town. Radio communication, not always reliable in the hilly country, was re-established with the tanks and Battalion HQ, and telephone lines were run out to the forward platoons. They were on watch for Jerry counter-attacks and I got them organised with clear fields of fire and fixed lines. But no attempt was made to retake the town.

I recall returning from the platoons and parking the company Jeep outside the villa, just as an A Echelon lorry pulled up with a cook and a driver who started unloading bundles of stores. They worked silently and fast, spurred on by an understandable desire not to linger unnecessarily in a dangerous spot so near the front line. The area would soon change. As always in the wake of the infantry and exploiting its success came brigade's sappers with Bailey bridges and mine detectors; then artillery, armoured units, petrol tankers and supply trucks; later would come the HQ groups, the field hospitals, the store depots, the mobile workshops— all the paraphernalia of a mechanised army on the move. What had so recently been a front line would become a safe and comfortable rear area, where staff officers could study their plans and men grumble if disturbed from their attempts to be as decently idle as they could be with impunity.

We were at Castelfiorentino for three days. Graham got permission from Russell to push on in what was becoming a race to be the first Eighth Army unit to reach the Arno. Ten kilometres to our right, 21 Brigade and the New Zealanders were advancing in Val di Pesa; further east, the 24th Guards Brigade and the 6th South African Armoured Division were in the Chianti hills and would be soon within sight of the great dome of Florence Cathedral. We were heading for Empoli, 25 kilometres west of Florence.

On a dusty white road beyond Castelfiorentino we surprised some Jerries who ran away leaving Teller mines scattered beside holes that had just been dug. This road seemed to offer a short cut so we followed it. The scenery was entrancing, with orchards and cornfields in the valleys, vines on the hills, clusters of umbrella pines and avenues of cypress trees leading to Renaissance villas. There was the luxury of feasting on almonds and fruit, abundant in that fertile land. But it was a deceptive Arcadia, disturbed without warning by the whistle and crash of artillery and stuttering bursts of spandau fire. Then Jerry would scarper and silent, golden Tuscany would bewitch again us as if nothing had happened.

Bivouacs were set up in the shade of olive groves. Under camouflage netting we would spread out maps and aerial reconnaissance photographs on the bonnets of our Jeeps and plan the next day's advance. We would eat, chat and smoke in the gloaming. A sentry's sudden challenge would provoke a chorus of Italian—partisans, the guerrilla fighters who became numerous as the war worsened for the Germans. They'd come in slowly, two by two, ducking under the olive branches. We'd give them food and quiz them for intelligence in the lingo we'd picked up. Orders for the next day were issued after dark, in my memory in moonlight, the harvest moon which shone on friend and foe alike. Then we would hear thuds of distant shellfire and see the glow of falling flares where the battle for Florence had begun, the eerie illumination flickering across the landscape onto our parked vehicles and faces as we stood watching quietly.

We were now at Monterappoli, on a ridge far ahead of other troops and dangerously exposed on our flanks. Our advance had been so rapid that our artillery couldn't keep up. The tankies were understandably reluctant to move forward into territory that we hadn't yet cleared. Scouts from C Company surprised a German patrol and one of our men was killed. The Jerries tried to surrender, changed their minds and ran into a row of vines where the Jocks shot two of them. One of our patrols, tipped off by partisans, captured seven Jerries resting in a house; another lost one man in a skirmish. We reached the slopes overlooking Empoli and the Arno plain. The distant peaks of the Apennines floated on the horizon above the late-afternoon haze. The next morning, 29 July 1944, A and C companies reached the flat ground on the southern outskirts of Empoli. Jerry tanks were reported in the area but none was seen. Between us and the Arno, the enemy had demolished buildings, mined and booby-trapped the ground and blocked the road under the Florence to Pisa railway tracks, west of the station where fires were burning merrily. Positions were established along the line of the railway. As usual, the station area had been bombed and we could see several large craters in which we suspected spandaus were concealed. C Company stole round the eastern flank, crossed the railway and followed a tributary of the Arno. At midnight the Jocks reached the river, the first Eighth Army unit to do so.

A Company established an OP in the tower of an abandoned cement plant on the south side of the tracks, east of the station. My company and the anti-tank platoon moved into line on the left flank, near the road under the train tracks. A Company was in the centre; C occupied orchards to the east; B was in reserve. Our mortar platoon was on the forward slopes of the foothills behind us. A Company's OP was not spotted by Jerry, so the CO used it to plan an attack. This was intended simply to let Jerry know that we had arrived in force. We would not to cross the river since one battalion was not sufficient to hold a bridgehead.

On the 31st a Canadian tank troop moved up behind the cement plant. Machine-guns were placed to fire point-blank into the enemy flanks. We synchronised watches and waited. Then our mortars opened fire. Bombs arced over our heads and exploded around the station and on the piazza behind it where some Jerry vehicles had been observed. The Shermans rumbled up to the railway tracks and fired every weapon they could bring to bear, and our machine-gunners picked off Germans as they ran away. The firefight was over in a few minutes. Ten Jerries were killed. There were no Argyll or Canadian casualties. There were similar engagements all along the front as the Eighth Army advanced to Florence and, on the Adriatic coast, to Ravenna.

The following day Brigadier Russell toured our positions, walking around with Graham, both men showing a commendable disregard for the occasional stonk. We were in quite a vulnerable position on a wide front into which the Germans could have counter-attacked, but our action at the station must have deterred them, as did our fighter-bombers buzzing across searching for targets. Both sides settled to reconnaissance and desultory exchanges of mortar fire. One Jerry stonk disturbed Battalion HQ behind the line, scattering men caught in the open and killing an unlucky corporal. The CO was outraged and came up to tell us to get the mortar, but its crew had moved position after firing. At dusk forays were made to the river to flush out enemy patrols, which had a habit of hiding by day in houses on the north bank and crossing at night to probe our defences. A subaltern was shot by mistake during a platoon change-over and died of wounds. In that instance it was not I who wrote the letter of condolence to the next of kin. Whoever did would have concealed the cause having been 'friendly fire'.

Up in the hills to our right a New Zealand patrol made a remarkable discovery. The Kiwis entered Montegufoni, a sixteenth-century villa. Inside the house they found groups of refugees, and a horde of Renaissance paintings from the Uffizi Gallery. The BBC's Wynford Vaughan Thomas and War Office PR writer Major Eric Linklater saw the treasures and broadcast the story, revealing that many artworks from the museums in Florence had been dispersed to the countryside for safety. We were expecting to take part in an assault on the city but Alexander ruled that out to save it from damage. The South African 6th Armoured Division, which liberated its southern neighbourhoods, was halted on banks of the Arno.

We left the front line for a rest area in the hills. It was obvious there had been more severe fighting in other sectors than we had experienced. Many of the villages we drove through were wrecked. In the piazza at Impruneta the church had been bombed and partly destroyed. The square was crammed with army trucks, tanks and sections of Bailey bridges, all soon to be deployed for the next push, the offensive on the Gothic Line. At our camp near Greve comic relief was provided when Will Fyffe arrived in a forces' entertainment unit Jeep. He was wearing a kilt, as he did in theatres at home where we were more used to seeing him perform. He and his troupe were invited to supper in the Officers' Mess. Chianti and nostalgia soon flowed. The party ended with a rousing chorus of Fyffe's most popular song, 'I Belong to Glasgow', echoing into the Tuscan twilight.

German rearguards began to pull out of Florence on 11 August, sniped at by partisans. The crackle of small-arms fire from street fighting continued for several days. The battalion took over from the 14th Sherwood Foresters at Bagno a Ripoli south-east of the city. Since the Arno was low and could be forded we sent a platoon across to the north bank to ferret around. Thanks to intelligence brought back our artillery shelled Jerry positions. Not in the city, though. That was forbidden on Alexander's orders. Three of my Jocks were wounded by return fire.

Battalion HQ was in a villa on a hill two kilometres from the river. One of the few perks in the campaign, for officers that is, was the power to commandeer the best properties. The villa's owner, Count Lamberti, was pleased to be of service and had a cellar of excellent wine. Ignoring sporadic shelling he pointed to the views from his garden: the Arno, the city's domes and campanili and the Apennines beyond. He pointed out the bridges dynamited by the enemy, except Ponte Vecchio which the German CO spared. The destruction was an inconvenience soon overcome by sappers who put a Bailey bridge across the river. On 23 August we were relieved by the 2nd Royal Scots and 1st Hertfordshires and left the count to his wine and the beautiful setting. At that moment Captain Rome had been questioning two women who had crossed through the lines from Florence and been nabbed by one of our patrols. It was well known that German intelligence sent Italian spies through our lines. The 'ladies' were, as Freddie Graham put it, of 'doubtful character'. We never found out quite what they were because we were shelled and moved out fast.

After Florence was liberated, Lieutenant-General Leese issued a personal message to be read out to all troops:

> You have won great victories . . . Now we begin the last lap. Swiftly and secretly, once again, we have moved right across Italy, an army of immense strength and striking power: to break the Gothic Line.

The Gothic Line was a menacing barrier across northern Italy. It ran along the Apennines from La Spezia in the west to Pesaro on the Adriatic coast. It had been constructed by German labour battalions since the fall of Rome. It was not a continuous barricade but a series of fortified ridges, mountain tops and passes, 25 to 50 kilometres deep, guarding the few main routes across the Apennines from the Arno to the river Po. The line was incomplete in August 1944 and should have been breached while the Germans were still disorganised, which was Alexander's intention. But because of the priority given to North-west Europe he did not have the resources in Italy for a rapid assault. The delay lost the Allies the best weather. Leese suggested a two-punch attack: the Eighth Army with a powerful right hook along the Adriatic coast to Ravenna and the Po valley, and the Fifth Army a left jab through the Apennines to Bologna. Leese expected the coastal punch would be the more effective. There were few roads in the mountains, the passes were well defended and the terrain would make it difficult to support out-flanking manoeuvres. He favoured a set-piece battle with artillery, tanks and infantry on the flat coastal ground. Alexander sold the plan to Clark by agreeing to lend him an Eighth Army corps to strengthen the push in the mountains.

The Eighth Army was switched secretly to the Adriatic coast, leaving behind the British 13 Corps (1st Infantry Division, 6th South African and 8th Indian divisions) which was placed under Fifth Army command. We were used to being moved around but not to an American sector. Leese's message had fine words, 'vital role, fresh honours', but I think it fair to say that by 1944 the morale of the old desert army was eroding. Our new role was preceded by the usual Operational Order, typed up and circulated to all officers. Those of us of all ranks with long service greeted those missives with cynical humour: 'Here we go again, the Agile and Suffering Highlanders.' So it was that on 31 August 1944 the battalion waded across a weir at Pontassieve and marched into the Mugello hills which the 8th Indian Division was ordered to capture as a prelude to the offensive.

It seemed that I might be promoted because Freddie Graham sent me on a course at the Company Commander's Tactical School at Benevento, where my former company commander, Bill Lossock, was an instructor. The course was a stroke of good fortune for me, because I missed the first major engagement the battalion had with the Germans on the Gothic Line, at the Battle of Monte Abetino on 2 September. It was a costly hill to take. Two officers were killed, two were wounded and two reported missing; nine Jocks were killed and 72 wounded or missing. I must say that if such statistics seem impersonal they were not always so. One of the dead was Major Jim Sceales. I had known him since Abyssinia. I met his father, General Sceales, ten years later at the Balaclava centenary celebrations at Stirling Castle. He questioned me about his son's death but I could tell him little. He was pleased when I said what a fine officer he had had been. The Germans buried him and put a wooden cross on the grave, which was found on the summit.

One of those missing was Major 'Rab' Caldwell who joined the battalion after Crete. In command of A Company he had gone forward on a recce with one of his platoon commanders, and a risky undertaking it proved to be. They ran into a patrol of Jerries wielding sub-machine guns. In the confusion the young subaltern managed to get away and hide in the undergrowth. There he lay with his heart in his mouth until the Germans gave up their search for him. When the coast was clear he made his way back to the battalion and reported what had happened. Rab was captured and, I learned later, spent the rest of the war as a PoW at Stalag 7 in Bavaria. I was well out of it on the course which was enjoyable and rewarding: lectures, demonstrations and tactical exercises by day, with all the comforts of a well-run mess in the evening. I must have impressed the commandant, Colonel Buchanan-Dunlop of the Cameronian Regiment, for he wanted me to join him on the staff of a tactical school he was being posted to in the UK. Tempting as that prospect was, and despite the colonel's inducement that he could wangle a home posting for me, my loyalties lay with the battalion. I turned down the offer.

9 The Gothic Line

Can the ordeals and sufferings of soldiers in the terrible conditions in the mountains on the Gothic Line be imagined? Not really. No one can imagine them, who had not been there and endured them through the worst Italian winter in living memory. Ground was gained not by massed assaults on broad fronts but hill by hill, pass by pass, foot by foot in countless isolated engagements, where leadership, courage and resilience determined success or failure. We had artillery support, but rarely from armour; both sides tried to deploy tanks in the mountains without much success. Low cloud prevented air strikes on enemy positions. The Gothic Line was an infantryman's war.

I returned from Benevento in mid-September 1944. The Argylls were camped north of Florence, in the midst of a hasty reorganisation after the Battle of Monte Abetino. I was promoted major and given command of A Company which I knew so well and had served with for so long. I had no illusions that the vacancy was the result of casualties and Caldwell's capture, or that I would be responsible for the well-being and leadership of 100 men. Many were replacements. Apart from Sanders, only a few of the Jocks in the three platoons had been with me in the Western Desert.

The camp was east of Borgo San Lorenzo in the foothills of the Apennines. Our brigade had been in reserve when the main offensive started on 13 September, with an artillery barrage that echoed for miles all along the Gothic Line. The Americans met with fiercer resistance than their attached British units experienced. The outer defences of the line were breached and the Allies advanced. On 21 September we received a warning order to move the next day to a concentration area at San Godenzo. I remember that because Major Oxborrow and Captain White had their leave in Florence cut short and because the weather turned for the worse. We entered the Sieve valley, leaving the Tuscany of olive groves and vineyards for inhospitable pine-clad hills. We stopped at Dicomano, which had been visited by American bombers earlier in the year. What remained had been blown up by the Germans. There was much activity: tanks and trucks rumbled in and out of ammo and petrol dumps, water points and workshops; soldiers hung around cookhouses, mobile bath units and tents; cigarettes were smoked, yarns exchanged, tea was brewed and tired limbs rested. When we arrived at our bivouac for the night we were greeted by the snorts and shuffles of 200 mules and their Indian muleteers, waiting to carry the battalion's food, ammo and equipment up the most tortuous stretch of our route to San Benedetto in Alpe.

Reveille was at 0500. We stood around smoking in quiet groups, stamping our feet and clutching mugs of piping hot tea as we prepared for a march into the mist. The muleteers checked their charges and their loads. At dawn we assembled and moved off, a long line of 600 Argylls on foot followed by the Indians with the animals. We passed through San Godenzo, a precipitous village blown to pieces by Jerry in an attempt to block the road. Only the church had been spared. We weaved up through the ruins, from where we faced 17 kilometres of hairpin bends rising to Passo del Muraglione, elevation 900 metres. Each time I looked back I saw our column snaking up below. The Apennines can be claustrophobic but when we reached the pass we were rewarded with a rest stop and a panorama of distant ridges floating above a layer of valley mist.

The road turned through a gap and spiralled down to San Benedetto, a dank hamlet in a gorge where our column made a left turn up a track which led to Marradi, 20 kilometres to the west. Other 8th Indian Division units had seized the ridges and cloud-covered summits on our left flank. But hills on the right were in enemy territory. Our task was to clear them to secure the route, which was muddy from rain which began to fall again. The basic rule of this type of warfare is to deny the heights to the enemy. Platoons leap-frogged one another from hill to hill. Battalion HQ, which someone without any desert experience had unwisely sited in a wadi, was washed away leaving the CO and his staff squelching knee-deep in mud. D company was driven off one hill, not by the enemy but by torrents of water. We spent the next couple of days patrolling dead-end valleys and knife-edge ridges. At one point, a Jerry machine-gun pinned down the whole company. That was a typical situation. In pouring rain that night, before we were obliged to locate and silence the spandau, we were very pleased to be relieved by an Indian unit. Formalities over, I sent the men down the muddy track and followed with the last platoon. The next day we passed an isolated monastery and saw spirals of wood smoke rise from Botteghette, a hamlet where we set up Battalion HQ and found billets while the men bivouacked nearby. We dried out for three days in the vast kitchens and commodious cellars of stone farmhouses. There was no electricity, just wood fires and oil lamps. The peasant women gave us what food they could spare and we shared our rations with them and their children. Cigarettes guaranteed the men's co-operation. We were in brigade reserve, but not for long.

Out billets were close to Marradi, a bomb-damaged town of tactical importance where the river Lamone and the road and railway between Florence and Faenza squeeze through a gap in the Apennines. It had been liberated on 24 September and its narrow streets and piazza were clogged with army vehicles and personnel. Our division was east of the town, waiting to help clear the hills above the Faenza road. On 3 October we received a warning order. At Popolano, a tumbledown hamlet two kilometres down the road, we got a good view of the Lamone valley and hills rising steeply on either side. The valley was exposed to enemy fire, so a direct approach would be costly. Major Taylor of the 14th Canadian said his tanks could give supporting fire but not risk being caught in the open because Jerry had SP (self-propelled) guns shelling the area. Brigadier Russell joined our confab. An infantry assault through the hills to the right of the road seemed to offer the best chance for success. Monte Cavallara, an 800-metre-high strongpoint was in the way. Until it was taken the advance of the whole brigade was stalled.

On 4 October Freddie Graham held a company commanders' conference at Battalion HQ. The Argylls would take over from the 6/13th Frontier Force Rifles and capture Monte Cavallara. Lieutenant-Colonel

Green, CO of the 6/13th, said his men had attacked it twice and been repulsed. It was vital, Graham emphasised, that it be taken 'at all costs'.

A Company was given the job.

I spent the evening with my platoon commanders, Captain White, Second Lieutenant Lindsay and Sergeant Taylor, at Company HQ, a dilapidated but watertight farmhouse. Lindsay was a newcomer, had never been in action. He seemed very low and full of foreboding.

'I don't think I'll survive this show,' he said.

White, in good spirits, countered, 'Don't be daft. You'll come through it all right. It'll be a walkover.'

We tried to cheer him up, partly to take our minds off the taboo he'd broken: we never let our feelings and fears show in that way. He had convinced himself his number was up. I was convinced I would come through the attack alive and well and survive the war. In any case, I was too concerned about my own duties and responsibilities to worry about what the Fates might have in store.

At 1100 the next morning we left the shelter of Botteghette and climbed through the woods, the CO and company commanders leading the way, to set up forward and battalion HQs. We separated to trek to our respective positions, single files of men one moment there, the next gone, only to reappear blundering further away on the steep hillsides. B and D companies hunkered down in valleys with an Indian company which was attached to the battalion. Cavallara was only two kilometres east of Botteghette but we couldn't see it for other ridges in the way. Because of the terrain, and the fact that the relief had to be done in the dark to avoid enemy detection, it took us ten hours to complete the change-over with the 6/13th. A sinister silence lay over the scene, broken occasionally by the crack of flares bursting when night fell.

I awoke in a cloud of mist. As it eddied away our position was revealed. We were in slit trenches and sangars almost level with a precipitous scrubby ridge which curved away for a kilometre either side of Monte Cavallara, its highest point, about 300 metres away. Gullies plunged from the ridge with some tree cover. There were four significant features, identified by their height in metres: Point 756 was held by A Company; Point 759, 250 metres to my right, by C Company; Point 744, Monte Cavallara itself and Point 685, on the south curve of the ridge 300 metres from the peak, were held by the enemy. Jerry was jumpy. A and C companies were shelled and one of my men was killed and another wounded.

Graham studied an aerial reconnaissance photograph of the area and went out to check a wadi on the north-west side of the ridge, up which an attack might be mounted, and briefed me. He had decided against a direct assault along the ridge where the two previous attacks had failed. The plan was simple: A Company to move to thick scrub at foot of the wadi by first light; C Company (Oxborrow) to engage enemy with mortars; artillery to provide diversionary fire; C Company smoke bombs to cover A Company's attack. Back at Point 756 I crawled into Company HQ's trench and sketched our assault route on a copy of the air photograph and briefed the platoon commanders. We synchronised watches and drank each other's health with a tot of rum. Final checks were made of weapons, ammo, rations and equipment and we settled down for the night. It rained intermittently and we sought what shelter we could, wrapped in our gas capes.

We woke before dawn. Platoon commanders passed round a rum ration and cigarettes to the men who sat quietly holding their rifles, waiting.

I checked my watch. 0500.

'Okay lads, this is it. Good luck. Let's go!'

As quietly as we could, we went down the hillside to the starting point in the wadi where we were unobserved from above.

0700. 7 October 1944.

The artillery and mortar concentration erupted. Explosions and smoke straddled the ridge. I gave the command: 'Company will advance!'

It was a three-platoon attack: Taylor on the right, Lindsay on the left and White in the centre. Company HQ, being me, the CSM, Sanders, a signaller and stretcher bearers followed. I'll never forget the cheerful, confident thumbs-up I got from Sergeant Taylor. He was a reliable regular soldier who had been posted to us from another battalion.

We got off to a bad start. A stray mortar salvo from C Company fell amongst us. One of the bombs, which failed to explode, struck my signaller and put him out of action. Luckily, the radio carried in a haversack was undamaged. Sanders knew how to operate it, strapped it on and secured the microphone round his neck. As he did so the three attacking platoons, having fanned out in the wadi, charged the hill. The mortars and artillery ceased firing and C Company's bombs began to fall, covering the summit in clouds of smoke. As we in Company HQ struggled up the slope it became clear that there was a fierce fight up ahead. Sounds of confused shouting came through the smokescreen, and the rattle of machine-gun and small-arms fire. Gasping for breath at the top I found the position cleared of Germans, the remnants of whom had withdrawn to positions further down and beyond the ridge.

0730. The hill was ours, but at a cost.

It was clear that all three platoons had casualties. We had already passed some walking wounded on their way down the hill to the regimental aid post, but at the top bodies lay about everywhere, some Germans, but mostly Jocks. The stretcher-bearers had their work cut out, picking them up and tending the wounded. Two of my platoon commanders had been killed, and the third wounded, and there was scarcely an NCO left alive or unscathed.

Taylor had led his platoon with great dash and courage, and though wounded was foremost in the attack, shouting encouragement and tossing grenades. He was evacuated, never returned to the battalion and, to my regret, I never saw the brave fellow again. Lindsay was dead, killed while leading his men, firing a Bren gun from the hip. I was shocked and saddened to see White among the wounded. He had received a burst of machine-gun fire in the body and was lying semi-conscious, his mangled guts spilling out on the ground. I carried two water bottles, one filled with water, the other with rum. I gave him a swig of rum, which I hope brought him some comfort in his dying moments, and left him to the care of the stretcher-bearers. More urgent duties had to be done. The men were in a bad way, demoralised by the carnage and the deaths of two popular officers. I had to revive their fighting spirit in case Jerry counter-attacked. Sergeant McKeown, one of the two senior NCOs who had not become casualties, kept a cool head and was a great help at that critical time. Lance Corporal Callaghan roused and encouraged his section and I promoted him on the spot. By 0830 we had consolidated our position. We had three prisoners, but they refused to talk so I sent them under escort to Battalion HQ. As the smoke and mist began to clear we came under machine-gun fire from Jerry's back-up position, Point 685. We kept our heads down in a hollow but the enemy fire was a nuisance, preventing free movement and observation. The spandau had to be spotted and put out of action.

I set off armed with grenades and a tommy gun, cautiously working my way from cover to cover along the ridge. I took Sergeant Pate with me, leaving McKeown in charge of what was left of the company. Pate, like McKeown, was a Glasgow man who had been with A Company since 1941 and through the campaigns in Eritrea, the Western Desert and Sicily. He wasn't over-anxious to come with me but as things turned out he didn't regret it. We didn't spot the spandau. It spotted us. A rattling burst of fire sent us scuttling for cover. Pate got a bullet in the foot. After recovering from the initial shock he could barely conceal his relief. His wound was minor, but enough to put him out of action. I'm afraid I didn't show him much sympathy, not that he wanted any, as I pulled out a field dressing. Keeping out of Jerry's line of fire, I helped him limp back to the company's position, then cursed inwardly as I watched him hobble down to the safety of the first aid post. Another NCO gone from my much-reduced company.

Pate and I had been so intent on stalking the spandau that neither of us heard the cries of some wounded men lying out of sight over the crest of the hill, one of them moaning for his 'mammy'. I crawled up to the edge of our position to see where they were. No sooner had I put my head over the top than there was a burst from the spandau. A volley of bullets hit the ground in front of my face. I tumbled back and lay still. Everyone thought I had been hit, but I was only blinded temporarily by the dirt thrown into my eyes. Any attempt at rescue the poor fellows lying outside would have been suicidal. They must have been far gone, for their cries soon ceased. I could see the effect of this on my men's faces. Sanders managed to rustle up some makeshift snacks and tea, a blessing that calmed us all. Then came the first blistering mortar stonk. I was on the radio to Battalion HQ at that moment, reporting to George Rome, who was now the adjutant.

'There's another one. Did you hear that?' I yelled into the mike, to leave him in no doubt about our situation. The stonk went on for some time. The Jocks were not only shaken but also infuriated and, had they been given the order, would have rushed the Jerry position, but more mortar fire kept our heads down. I had another miraculous escape, when a young Jock, crouching next to me, got a bomb splinter in the neck that almost decapitated him and he bled to death. Our situation was sufficiently vulnerable for Russell, who came up from Division HQ at midday, and Graham to act. Two B Company platoons were ordered to attack Point 685 through our position. Eventually they turned up at 1600, to be greeted with some derisive banter: 'We've done our bit, boys. Finish the buggers off and get that fucking mortar.' I felt that it was about time some others had a taste of what we had been through.

Seeing our sorry state, B Company's Jocks were not to be too keen to get the mortar. They were shaken too, when another stonk fell amongst us just as they were assembling to go over the top. Their officers and NCOs did their best to restore order. It was vital that there be no delay because C Company's mortars were firing on Point 685 to cover the attack. The leading platoon went over the top, accompanied by our shouts of encouragement and covering fire. I was put out at seeing their company commander berating some reluctant heroes and pushing and kicking them over the edge. I felt he would have done better to go over himself and shame them into following him. Both platoons surged on and overran Point 685 after a fierce fight. Jerry counter-attacks were beaten off, then all was quiet. I stood contemplating the body of a young German. I salvaged some of his belongings: identification and family photographs, the usual stuff. I was filled with sombre thoughts about the untimely deaths of so many young men, on both sides, whose lives had been sacrificed, and wondered how many more were to die. None of us had much sleep that night and what little I had was interrupted by disturbing dreams.

At dawn I sent a patrol out into the mist. There was no sight or sound of Jerry whose casualties included their company commander, killed by our artillery. That was small consolation for our losses. The attacks by A and B companies had cost 15 men killed and 44 wounded. Of those, two officers and ten other ranks killed and 20 wounded were A Company men. The dead were laid to rest at a makeshift cemetery in a pine grove at Vonibbio, a nearby hamlet. Padre Dow conducted a brief ceremony at which a piper played the lament.

The day after the battle we got our first hot meal for ages and a chance to wash, shave and tidy ourselves up. The brigade's gunners set up an OP on Point 744. Just another hill for them, thanks to the poor bloody infantry. Graham came up with Russell and Dobree. Russell said that our 'very excellent performance' had enabled the 3/8th Punjabis to force the enemy off the next strongpoint, aiding the advance of the brigade. We stayed on Monte Cavallara for several nights before we were relieved by Indians, the Jaipurs I recall. The Jocks of A and B Companies were exhausted and subdued as I led them down to Botteghette. There was a party in our honour: a hot meal, an extra beer ration for the men and whisky for the officers. Reaction to shattered nerves, relief that it was all over and thoughts about the men I'd lost overwhelmed me, and I couldn't enter into the spirit of things. I'd had little sleep for a week. I recall Shaw, who was second in command of D Company, bending over me and saying, 'Look at this, chaps, Ray's passed out like a light.' I slept round the clock.

When we got out of the front line I made a list of the casualties for the record, and because it was my duty to write letters of condolence to the next of kin. Those who replied did so with poignant words of faith and dignity characteristic of the times. I will not forget that day, when A Company seized the summit and took 30 percent casualties. It was not a big show, just a routine attack with a limited objective; wishful thinking by the brass to seek a breakthrough then in that part of the line. It was known to and remembered only by the men who took part.

On 15 October 1944 we formed up and marched to Marradi for transport to take us out of the line, to Borgo San Lorenzo for ten days of rest, leave and training. The casualties on Monte Cavallara made it necessary to amalgamate A and B companies as a temporary unit, A/B Company, which I was assigned to command. Second-in-command was B Company's Captain Graham Wood, who had trained at the OCTU at Dunbar shortly before I was there and had been overseas since 1940, as an IO at GHQ Cairo before joining the battalion in the Western Desert. We agreed the best thing about the brigade's rest area was the mobile bath unit, a godsend as normal standards of cleanliness and hygiene were impossible to maintain in the mountains. Then there was the bliss of crisp, fresh clothing and feeling clean and civilised after weeks in mud-stained battledress. We had Day Leave to Florence, 78 passes of which I got one.

The city of the Renaissance had been spared the worst of the war. The Uffizi Gallery was closed because of blast damage when the Arno bridges were blown, but the Duomo and Baptistry were open. Statuary outside the Palazzo Vecchio had shed its protective covers. Shops and street stalls were open. I bought postcards and a Uffizi catalogue. Army headgear bobbed to and fro: forage caps, bush hats, brass hats, tin hats, turbans, balmorals and glengarries. Military vehicles rumbled along the narrow streets or were parked in the piazzas. Florence was a through route to the mountains, and army signs—Arrow Route, Star Route, Sword Route— were everywhere. Many citizens were short of food and there was poverty and hardship. Buskers stood at street corners playing flutes or violins; ragged children, tiny figures lost in the wartime life of the city, hung around cafés scrounging for food. We lucky conquerors had a slap-up lunch at a Forces club in a palazzo whose frescoed salons had become an army canteen. Shaw and I engaged a fiacre to take us up to Piazzale Michelangelo, from where the panorama of the city looked like the prewar postcards I had bought. Dozens of Allied soldiers strolled around or had their photographs taken. Our driver stood smoking and chatting to colleagues. A few months earlier they had no doubt taken German officers up to view the same beauty spot.

Back at base I presided at a Court of Inquiry, following an accident while grenades were being primed on a training exercise. Through carelessness or incompetence by the NCO in charge, one of the grenades went off, killing one Jock and wounding two others. Such accidental deaths were few. Most of our casualties were caused by enemy action— bullet wounds, shrapnel from mortars and shellfire, and landmines. I had to hold Company Office, one of those out-of-the-line chores which I disliked. Some soldiers who were courageous and reliable in combat managed to fall foul of authority whenever relieved of the obligatory, life-saving discipline of the battlefield. Cases of Conduct Unbecoming, AWOL or minor breaches of regulations were common. 'How many have we got?' I would ask CSM Stewart. He'd brief me on each case, march the offender in and then stand to attention beside me. On one occasion three Jocks had been arrested, fighting drunk, by Military Police while on a day trip to Florence. Nobody had been hurt in the affray, a street fight with a bunch of Yanks. I asked them who won.

'We did, sir.'

'Save it for Jerry,' I said and dismissed them.

The CSM reported that one of my subalterns, in charge of a leave party on a day trip to the city, had failed to turn up at the rendezvous the night before and missed the truck bringing the men back. Furthermore, he had not returned by breakfast time. He was one of several misfits posted to the battalion as replacements and had already fallen foul of me by his behaviour. At first I was inclined to be tolerant of someone who was young and inexperienced and knew nothing of life in an infantry battalion. Yet his admitted ambition was to kill Germans and it was no secret that he coveted medals. His Jocks called him 'Holy Willie' because of a book he carried which they mistook for a Bible but was actually a manual of infantry tactics. He was a square peg in a round hole. If one could have been found, his men would gladly have thrown him into it. He antagonised his sergeant and NCOs. I'd already challenged him about his hectoring manner and told him to go easy with his platoon, after his sergeant had complained about being bawled out in front of the men. I told him it would be wise to keep on the right side of the sergeant, who was a good soldier and could help him, and that the men had been through a rough time. I said they might not seem as keen as he would like them to be but that they would do what was wanted of them when the time came, if he treated them fairly.

He burst into Company Office unannounced and stood in front of me, dishevelled and distraught.

'Reporting back, sir,' he stammered. 'Got lost. Most terribly sorry about this. Let you down. Came to report as soon . . .'

'Get out of here. I'll hear your explanation later,' I roared.

I asked Graham to take him off my hands. D Company was short of a junior officer. The CO said I'd have to make out an official report. I didn't want to damn the man completely, so he stayed. Some of the newcomers were straight off the boat; others were ack-ack gunners, artillery chaps or older rear-echelon men, unfit and untrained. These replacements were common towards the end of the Italian campaign, as the Allies were short of infantry and we were not a strategic priority.

The Allies' autumn offensive in the Apennines had met with limited success. The Germans resisted for a time, then it became clear that they were following an all too familiar pattern. Positions would be captured at great cost, then Jerry would withdraw to more prepared defences, and the same tactics would have to be repeated across the ravines and ridges that obstructed our advance, which crept forward slowly.

On 25 October the battalion went back into the mountains. For the next two months we were moved around to relieve other units, never knowing where we might be sent or what to expect. In the first week of November it snowed. We were in the Marradi sector, at Popolano, as 19 Brigade's reserve on Sword Route. The river Lamone was a torrent. The valley dissolved in the distance to the north, where lay the vast plain of the river Po, our destination, eventually. At least we had dry billets in village houses and farms. We made forays down the valley or into the hills. Enemy shelling was infrequent and patrol activity almost non-existent.

Not so the snow, sleet or rain, which persisted for days on end. Jeeps and Bren carriers slithered and spun up to a dead-ends way off the main road, where we'd rendezvous with Sepoys waiting with mules. Neither the animals nor their handlers got much sympathy—we were no better off ourselves, being but beasts of burden like them at times. Our only benefit was that we qualified for a 'high altitude ration' which gave us extra tea, sugar, milk and chocolate, and a daily issue of rum.

A/B Company plugged a gap in the front line between the 6/13th and 1/12th Frontier Force battalions; relieved the 1/5th Mahrattas and 3/15th Punjabis in the hills; secured an undamaged railway bridge near San Cassiano, a miserable, soaking village eight kilometres down the valley. In mid-November we were relieved by the 6/13th. There followed another brief respite at Popolano. Then we were back at San Cassiano, thought to be unoccupied, but when A/B Company probed the road several partisans appeared and told us that Jerry had some SP guns in the village, although we hadn't seen them or been shelled. We were on the other side of a blown bridge. It was case of live and let live, and the Germans didn't seem eager to cause any trouble. The main threat was mines and booby traps. We knew to tread warily and take with a pinch of salt assurances of sappers that tracks were safe. I remember picking my way along one taped track supposedly cleared, when one of the men in front of me trod on a Schu mine which blew his foot off. D Company in the hills lost three men in one day, all to landmines.

A/B Company stayed on the edge of the village while the rest of the battalion occupied hilltop positions on a two-kilometre front directly east. Most of the houses were in a bit of a mess as a result of shellfire. The Germans had also been thorough in their destruction and looting. I did a spot of the latter myself. One house I went into was almost completely ransacked, scarcely a stick of furniture left. Chopped up for firewood I expect. Anything else of value had been spirited away. Other contents were scattered around. Among them I found some opera scores and art books which I felt no compunction about taking, and treasured for many years after the war. The weather improved briefly and there was so little activity that the CO organised a pheasant shoot with some Italians, who turned out to be alarmingly trigger-happy. When he got back he said the hunt had been 'a more dangerous sport than chasing the Boche'.

At the end of the month we got a warning order to assist the 6th Armoured Division in the Santerno river valley. As usual, we company commanders took a couple of Jeeps and set out for a recce, 20 kilometres as the crow flies but for us a bone-rattling 40 kilometres via Castel del Rio on an atrocious mountain road which twisted and climbed into the cloud base. When we got to the 6th Armoured HQ we were told that things were under control. Exasperated, we drove back, to find that the orders had been cancelled. Battalion HQ then received another urgent summons. This one was not a false alarm.

We were sent to reinforce 2nd Brigade, 1st British Infantry Division which was east of Route 65, the main Florence to Bologna highway. The Fifth Army had been stopped in this sector by the enemy and the weather. After liberating Marradi, 1st Division had relieved the US 88th Division and was now holding a vital part of the line. On 3 December we approached Frassineto, an isolated hilltop hamlet. The three-kilometre climb to it, with mules hauling equipment from the jeep-head, began at dusk and took five hours. The battalion took over from the 6th Gordon Highlanders on a two-kilometre-long mountain. There were two 600-metre summits—Monte Grande furthest west and Monte Cerere to the east—linked by a ridge. Slightly below and just east of Monte Cerere was Frassineto where we were billeted. The 3/8th Punjab Regiment and 6/13th Frontier Force Rifles took over positions on Monte Grande and Monte Cerere respectively. The Canadians of the 14th Armoured stayed at Marradi because the terrain, weather and condition of the roads prevented their tanks being deployed.

We awoke to see a valley to the north and a final roll of hills occupied by the Germans barring the way to Bologna, 20 kilometres north-west. If the weather had been clear we might have seen the domes and towers of the city. Behind us in the San Clemente valley was 1st Division's HQ and base area, which was crowded with camps, supply dumps, maintenance depots and vehicles. The front was thinly manned and vulnerable. A retreat from San Clemente would be a serious setback. Facing us was 3rd Battalion, 1st Parachute Regiment, the para boys of the 1st Parachute Division. The Argylls knew them well from Crete and the Gustav Line. We were about to get to know them better.

Frassineto was a group of houses and farm buildings at the end of a north-east-facing spur in full view of the German positions. It stuck out like a sore thumb. And like any sore thumb it attracted more than its fair share of hard knocks. These came from artillery shells, machine-gun bullets and mortar bombs. Worst of all was the fire from an 88. This gun damaged most of the buildings we occupied. The spur was open on both flanks and exposed at the front, which made movement impossible in daylight. The only safe place to be was in the cellars.

The battalion's precarious position was no more than 500 metres square. I was in command of A/B Company at Frassineto on the end of the sore thumb. C Company and forward HQ were in dugouts and slit trenches on the knuckle; D Company was at the wrist, at Casa Nuova, a farm on a rise below the summit of Monte Cerere. The enemy-held road from the valley below us was 'tankable' and had to be watched by two A/T crews. Despite the proximity of our positions, the lie of the land and Jerry observation meant we could reach each other only by dangerous or circuitous routes along steep tracks. Slit trenches filled with mud and water which froze at night. In the open, with only one blanket per man, conditions were grim. I recall getting on the radio to Battalion HQ to complain, contrasting our sorry state with the relative comfort at HQ behind the lines where I knew there were blankets galore. More came up from San Clemente on the next mule train. Brigadier Dobree visited us and declared that we had to dig in, as if we didn't know.

A/B Company HQ was in the substantial cellar of a shell-shattered farmhouse where I spent most of the daylight hours in a constant fug of cigarette smoke, fumes from the fire, oil lamps and cooking. Each evening I would button up my leather jerkin and prepare for my nightly round. The round was necessary because Jerry shelling disrupted field telephone lines and our radios were unreliable. It was also vital for morale that the men see their company commander out in the forward positions. I'd find them huddled in their slit trenches gripping their rifles with numb fingers, gazing out alert for enemy patrols. I'd give them a few words of encouragement or share a sardonic comment and move on. It was always a chancy business. There were many incidents in the mist. Shaw sent out a patrol but it was spotted. Jerry charged and one of D Company's men was killed and three taken prisoner in the ensuing scrap. An enemy patrol clashed with a D Company post and was repelled with grenades, which wounded one of the Jerries who lay moaning out of sight. He was dragged in but died before he could be interrogated. A Jerry deserter came through our lines. He wouldn't talk except to say that when we were captured we didn't say much so why should he, cheeky blighter.

A/B Company spent a week out on the sore thumb. That was considered enough and we were mighty pleased when our turn came to be relieved, by C Company. We were a sorry-looking lot when we came off that dreaded spur, bleary-eyed, muddy, unshaven and unwashed. We moved only a couple of hundred metres, to forward HQ below Casa Nuova. At least it was in a relatively safe spot, even though it was exposed and we only had dugouts for shelter. We barely had time to settle in.

0700. 12 December 1944.

We were shaken by a German attack. It came out of the blue, through a thick mist at dawn. The whole of the brigade's front line was shelled.

At that moment I was in my dugout, stark naked and enjoying the luxury of a thorough wash, the first for a week. Shouts and machine-gun and small-arms fire were coming from Casa Nuova. Mortar bombs thudded. I scrambled into my clothes. I couldn't see a thing in the smoke and mist but I shouted to the signaller to get Battalion HQ on the radio. I still remember how simple sounds were curiously magnified in the throbbing air: the crackle of the radio; the sporadic shouts in the mist. We were in a tight corner.

D Company's forward platoon was overrun, with some men killed and others captured. Casa Nuova was attacked, and Frassineto. Jerry assaults on the Indians' positions were successful, initially. The 6/13th's forward platoon was forced back from the flanks of Monte Cerere. Another Jerry foray was directed to the tip of the Frassineto thumb, where paras rushed uphill through a smoke-screen but were driven back by C Company's Bren and mortar fire. D Company's forward HQ at Casa Nuova was overrun. My weary men realised the danger and, like the good soldiers they were, they buckled to and prepared themselves. For all we knew, as we peered out into the void, we ourselves might be rushed by the para boys. That didn't happen but we came under steady fire from Casa Nuova.

I shouted orders to organise a sound defensive position, putting on a show of calm confidence, as did my platoon commanders and the NCOs. Holy Willie put up a good show and began to earn my respect and that of his men by showing coolness under fire and organising his platoon efficiently. In fact he was in his element. He was so eager to get to grips with Jerry that he kept urging me to let him rush the Germans with his platoon. I couldn't allow that, as we had been ordered to hold our ground. In any case his Jocks would probably have mutinied had he tried. The 6/13th counter-attacked and broke the enemy's grip on Monte Cerere. The para boys at Casa Nuova, who ran up to stem the retreat, were caught in the open by machine-gun fire. By mid-morning dead and wounded Jerries lay all over the place. Their CO, according to a radio intercept, reported that if he wasn't reinforced he'd have to withdraw.

Encouraged by this and the courage of the 6/13th, Graham ordered D Company's reserve platoon to counter-attack. This order only got through because Shaw's signaller had repaired field telephone lines while under fire. Every mortar in the battalion then plastered the enemy positions for over half an hour. D Company's men leaped from cover and dashed across a stretch of open ground to recapture Casa Nuova. We gave covering Bren fire and a blast from a Piat anti-tank gun. I still remember following the flight of the hurtling bomb as it flew straight through a window of the farmhouse and burst with a shattering explosion inside. That had a great effect, causing the Germans to panic. They were on the point of withdrawing when the D Company platoon rushed them, taking three prisoners, and found five paras killed by the Piat bomb. All along the line the Germans were repulsed with heavy losses.

The following morning some Jerry smoke bombs hit Frassineto as we stood-to, but no attack came. Later, we were bombarded by a high-velocity gun fired from a very long range. Its shells came in like an express train, hitting the ground and scattering shrapnel, stones and mud across 100 metres, leaving huge craters. As always, such events recorded for the battalion's War Diary were understated—'Shelling on A/B Company was highly unpleasant', the adjutant or CO wrote. On our last day at Frassineto two Jocks were killed when that one-in-a-hundred chance hit demolished the house they were sheltering in.

We were on Monte Cerere for 15 days, on edge all the time and pretty numb from the experience. On 17 December we were relieved by 2nd Battalion, the Sherwood Foresters. The descent from that mountain was the worst I ever made. The tracks were in an appalling state. Not just knee deep in mud but at times waist deep. Several men got stuck and had to be hauled out. As the last platoon blundered in the dark, the rain streaming off our faces, I heard the corporal yell at a Jock in front, 'Hey Jimmy. Where the fuck's the Bren?'

The Jock, who'd either lost the gun or left it behind, swivelled round, knee-deep in mud, bristling with anger and frustration.

'Where the fuck's the Bren? Fuck the fucking Bren, the fucking fucker's fucked!'

What a release of tension that was.

After four days' rest in the base area we were interrupted by move orders, cancellations and abortive recces of new positions. At one jeep-head, where we were to relieve the South Staffordshire Regiment, we were welcomed by a blistering mortar stonk. Their positions were under constant Jerry observation, another Frassineto with farm buildings battered by the same long-range gun. The South Staffs' CO had been pinned down in his forward HQ for a fortnight. As Freddie Graham put it, 'We looked around at each other in grim despair while the mortar bombs thudded outside.' Happily for us, a message from Brigade came through: 'Recce parties Argylls rejoin battalion forthwith'. We skedaddled as fast as we dared, to Castel del Rio and then back to Borgo San Lorenzo. The battalion was gone when we returned. Another order was waiting. It took us to the Serchio valley where 19 Brigade was sent urgently halfway across Italy to support the US 92nd Division. We camped outside Lucca where we were put on three-hours' readiness on Christmas Day. The 92nd, the only black American frontline division in Europe, had only arrived in Italy in August and was not expected to put up much resistance to a determined attack. It was strung out on a 30-kilometre front near Barga, below the snow-clad peaks of the Apuan Alps. Intelligence had warned of a German attack, which duly happened.

Boxing Day found us 20 kilometres up the Serchio valley. After long spells of fighting the enemy in harsh conditions my battle-weary Jocks didn't take kindly to this, especially as it meant coming to the aid of the Yanks. The 3/8th Punjabis led our advance; the 6/13th on the right; the Argylls on the left flank. When the 92nd came under fierce attack it was outclassed and outfought. If they didn't exactly turn and run they beat a hasty and disorderly retreat. Even our own forward positions had to make a more orderly withdrawal to take up stronger positions further back. My own company didn't see any action and the battalion suffered no casualties. Jerry, faced with stiffer opposition and American reinforcements, gave up the attack, which in any case had only limited objectives, and withdrew to the north.

We enjoyed a peaceful spell in the Lucca/Pisa area, a cushy sector. The weather had improved with crisp, clear frosty air and the first sunny skies we had seen for weeks. Major-General Russell had promised Graham that we would be back at Lucca in time for Hogmanay and we were. Russell and Dobree visited Battalion HQ. The Pipes and Drums paraded in Lucca, and at Pisa in the campo at the Leaning Tower. The tower had survived recent fighting. Lucca was unravaged by the war. The CO passed on news that A Company's awards for the Battle of Monte Cavallara had come through. I was awarded the Military Cross (Immediate Award). My recommendations of Sergeant Taylor for a Distinguished Service Medal and five other NCOs and men for the Military Medal were approved. I still regret that I didn't put Sanders in for an award. I felt that had I done so it would have been looked on by the men as favouritism, and thus resented.

Despite the good weather and being out of the line, I was feeling pretty low. Battle fatigue and general war weariness, I suppose. To add to my low spirits some officers, including my old friend Shaw, were granted a month's leave by air to the UK, and 24 men who had been overseas for four and a half years left for Naples and a ship home. It seemed I'd have to soldier on until the end of the war. I spoke to Freddie Graham who, being the good CO he was, recognised my symptoms. He sent me off to Rome on a week's leave. The break must have done me some good, for I came back refreshed and rejuvenated if not exactly spoiling for a fight. Graham left by air for home leave on 5 February 1945. He rejoined the battalion at the end of the month in time to lead it to victory. We knew a big push was coming but few of us foresaw the massive might of the Allied war machine, or that the Argylls' role would be a vital and terrifying ordeal.

10 The Last Battle

While we were in the Apennines the Eighth Army had breached the Gothic Line on a 25-kilometre front on the Adriatic coast, in September 1944. Ravenna fell on 4 December and Faenza on the 16th. By January 1945 the Allies were not only in the hills above Bologna but also had advanced from the Adriatic coast to the river Senio, a strongly fortified line in the Po valley held by the German Tenth Army. Lieutenant-General Leese had expected the coastal plain would suit his tanks, artillery and air support but he had not anticipated the weather. As in the mountains, the advance was slow and everything ground to a halt in the face of dogged German resistance and winter rains. Leese was replaced by Lieutenant-General Richard McCreery, also a veteran of the Western Desert. McCreery's job was to prepare for a spring offensive that would destroy the German forces in Italy.

The 8th Indian Division was sent by devious route via Florence and Perugia to the Adriatic coast to rejoin the Eighth Army. February 1945 saw the Argylls at Porto San Giorgio, 200 kilometres south of the front line. Our division was preparing to take over from the Canadians, who were about to be transferred to North-west Europe. Like any seaside resort in winter San Giorgio was a dismal place and the weather was nasty. We were not unhappy to move up to Russi in the Po valley to prepare for the big push. North of Pesaro we passed through remnants of the previous offensive, in a zone of battlefield wreckage such as I had not seen since the Western Desert.

The Po valley was a complete contrast to the claustrophobic mountains where we had been for so long. Here was a plain of big skies and wide horizons, threaded with irrigation canals and tributaries of the mighty river Po. The land was cultivated yet austere, often hidden in morning fog. The roads were mostly single track and often ran along the tops of dykes with few passing places. They were either muddy or dusty, depending on the weather, and clogged with traffic. Even the arrow-straight Route 9 from the coast to Bologna could not cope with the build-up of tanks, heavy vehicles and field guns. Stone farmhouses appeared every few hundred metres. The larger estates had barns and the landowner's house built around courtyards. These farms and villages provided comfortable billets at our various staging posts around Russi, a compact country town, inward-looking like them all, centred around a piazza and church.

The battalion relieved the Royal 22nd Regiment, the French-Canadian 'Van Doos', at Russi on 28 February. They were in reserve and soon left for Livorno and a ship to Marseilles (as did our former armoured support, the 14th Canadian Armoured Regiment). After the change-over we went into the front line, between the rivers Lamone and Senio. It was reckoned to be a quiet sector. Quiet, except for a fusillade of rockets fired by multi-barrelled mortars which fell in the A/B Company area with an unearthly, wailing roar. The rockets landed six at a time but they did little damage on the open ground and caused no casualties, that time. We got used to the 'Moaning Minnies' when we realised that mere noise wouldn't harm us. We were pulled out after a week and rested for a few days, then tramped forward again to relieve the 3/8th Punjabis in a position at the Senio.

Like the Lamone, the Senio flowed north-east from the Apennines and entered the Adriatic north of Ravenna. Where it crossed the Po floodplain it was channelled along a dyked, man-made watercourse, more a canal than a river, with a line of floodbanks either side. They were a formidable barrier. They stretched across the plain like railway embankments. These raised banks blocked our view and progress, with steep slopes on both sides rising to the height of the farm buildings and three-storey villas we sheltered in. A pathway five metres wide ran along the top of each bank. Between the banks was a 30-metre-wide gap, at the bottom of which was the river. Now that the rains had eased the river was only few metres wide, a metre deep and flowed slowly. The banks, however, were honeycombed with enemy dugouts and machine-gun posts. Any incursion to the top of the near bank exposed us to enemy fire from the far one. The Germans also held parts of the near bank. Both banks were strung with barbed wire and sewn with mines.

A/B Company was based at a farm 100 metres from the river, with forward positions close to and on the near bank. D Company was 100 metres to our left at another farmhouse. C Company, two sections of A/B Company, our A/T platoon, machine-gunners and mortars were 500 metres behind. Because we were so close to the enemy, moving about in daylight was hazardous, except in the morning mist and then only on marked tracks. Enemy listening posts received any movement or talk on our side of the floodbanks. We were under constant surveillance, our forward position isolated in daylight and unapproachable from the rear except at night. Water, food and ammo were brought in after dark, and field telephone lines severed by Jerry stonks repaired overnight. Every night saw an exchange of grenades, like First World War trench warfare. We tossed over far more than we received which suggested that the Germans were running short of ammo.

There were two abandoned farmhouses between my position and D Company. Jerry had a habit of slipping across the Senio at night to occupy these buildings and sniping at us during the day. To stop this I got our sappers to mine the two buildings. A satisfying explosion followed. The second charge failed to detonate but the sappers went back and blew the building the next night. By day we were often stonked by mortars and Moaning Minnies. D Company was unlucky. Six of its men were killed and seven wounded by mortars. Three more were killed when a rocket hit their farmhouse. We also got Jerry propaganda leaflets intended for our Indian comrades, sent over in canisters fired by artillery. These contained a crude and completely ineffective message:

To Indian troops. You are helping a foreign nation which for the last
200 years has enslaved you.

The Indians were fully aware that enslavement was the Nazis' plan, not ours. Our own propaganda, signed by Alexander, offered safe conduct for PoWs or deserters. One evening two Jocks brought in a Jerry. He was shaking and demoralised and talked after a drink. He seemed quite pleased to be captured and said that he'd have been shot by his officer had he been caught leaving his post. He told our IO that the near bank was mined, wired and booby-trapped. We had already discovered that. But he also revealed that it would be abandoned for the far bank if attacked strongly. He said that the Germans had very little fuel for their vehicles and armour; that trucks, panzers and SP guns were almost immobilized and senior officers' cars had been adapted to run on gas. All their other transport was horse- or bullock-drawn.

Back at Russi Freddie Graham had resumed command of the battalion. Majors MacFie and Wood were repatriated. Reinforcements arrived. A/B company was disbanded. I retained command of A Company with Scott-Barrett, now a captain, as my second-in-command. Shaw was promoted Major and given command of B Company which was reinstated. By chance the 8th Argylls were billeted in Russi. The last time we had seen them was when we piped them ashore in Sicily. Graham invited their CO and officers to our mess. They had been in the Apennines north of Castel del Rio, suffered 120 casualties and were reduced to three companies. They spent Christmas out of the line, then moved to Monte Grande after we had been shifted to Lucca. It seemed that we got out just in time because the 8th Argylls were caught in sub-zero temperatures and heavy snow.

It was in Russi that Shaw and I were astonished to meet our old friend MacDougall, whom I had last seen in limbo at the IBD at Benevento. We were delighted to see that he had emerged from that setback still his old self and still a captain in the Argylls, but now attached to 1st Battalion, the London Scottish Regiment. Since August 1944 his battalion had taken part in the coastal offensive on the Gothic Line, had been in our Senio sector and was now in reserve near Cesena. He had driven over to Russi to find us. We contrived to meet again, at Faenza. I parked the company Jeep in the town's arcaded piazza, which had been knocked about by shelling and was now packed with army vehicles and soldiers. Mac knew his way around because the London Scottish, with New Zealanders and Gurkhas, had liberated Faenza in December. We had a jolly good drink together and a long talk as we brought each other up to date with our travels and adventures. We knew the war in Italy must be coming to an end and, having survived so far, we didn't relish the prospect of becoming a casualty at this late stage.

'See you in Sauchiehall Street,' I said to Mac.

'Aye, a better road and a better country than this,' he replied as we shook hands and drove away from that war-damaged piazza.

We spent the next few days in a rear area by the river Montone practising for the assault on the Senio. We grappled with portable assault boats and kapok bridging panels (floats to which a wood deck was attached, forming a footbridge). We trained with 'Ark' ramp carriers (driven into the river to allow following vehicles to cross on top of them) and an aggressive menagerie of tanks and armoured vehicles: 'Wasp' flame-throwing Bren carriers, 'Wolverine' tank destroyers, 'Scorpion' mine-clearing and 'Crocodile' flame-throwing tanks, 'Kangaroo' armoured personnel carriers and 'Buffalo' amphibious APCs. We got used to the sounds and sight of them clanking and crawling around in the morning mist like prehistoric monsters.

By the end of March the weather had improved and the Fifth and Eighth armies were resupplied, reinforced and reorganised. The Allies had overwhelming superiority in men, tanks, guns and aircraft, and they meant to use it to full advantage. The Fifth Army was ready to break out of the Apennines, head for Bologna and press north to the river Po, Verona and the Alps. The Eighth Army would smash the German line on the Senio and clear the way to Ferrara, the Po delta and Venice, with a secondary push on Route 9 to link up with the Americans, and an amphibious operation on Lake Commachio, a lagoon on the coast. The enemy's retreat across the plain would present easy targets for the Allied air forces and advancing armour.

At Battalion HQ Freddie Graham briefed company commanders. I can still hear the rustle that broke the silence in the farmhouse where we stood as he unrolled a map, produced air photographs and explained our part in the strategy. The Eighth Army's direct assault on the Senio was to be made in our sector by the 8th Indian and 2nd New Zealand divisions.

The 8th Indian Division's 19 Brigade with 1st Argylls was to be in the centre of the line. Graham paused, then turned to the Argylls' tactical role. At that point I realised that I would be the first over the top.

He handed out Orders of the Day and a minute-by-minute countdown to the Senio assault. A Company's task: neutralise the German forward defences and secure both sides of the near bank; B Company on the right and C Company on the left, pass through A Company to a point 200 metres beyond the far bank and deal with any further opposition; D Company ready in reserve; tanks of the North Irish Horse follow up, support the battalion on the far side of the river. The plan seemed simple and straightforward enough to those who made it. For the Jocks who had to see it through it was a different matter, at a time when we were war-weary. We accepted our fate with as much cheerfulness, stoicism and courage as we could muster.

Field Marshal Alexander's message was passed around:

Soldiers, Sailors and Airmen of the Allied Forces in the Mediterranean Theatre. Final victory is near. The German forces are now very groggy and only need one mighty punch to knock them out for good. The moment has now come for us to take the field for the last battle which will end the war in Europe . . . It will not be a walk-over; a mortally wounded beast can still be very dangerous. You must be prepared for a hard and bitter fight, but the end is quite certain, there is not the slightest shadow of doubt about that. You, who have won every battle you have fought, are going to win this last one . . . Godspeed and good luck to you all.

We moved into our assembly areas at dusk. Usually, each company was rotated to share the dangers of assault as well as the relative security in reserve. At the Battle of the Senio all four companies would be in action.

D-day was 9 April 1945. That morning heralded the most deafening day I have ever lived through.

At 1340 hours waves of Allied heavy bombers flew over, high in the sky, followed at intervals by hundreds of fighter-bombers at low level, plastering enemy artillery positions and reserve areas. We watched from trenches in our assembly areas where we waited, burdened with equipment, ration packs, entrenching tools, bridging gear, steel helmets and weapons and ammo with which we were expected to rush the near bank of the river. Directly after the air strikes came a four-hour artillery and mortar bombardment of the German defences. Clouds of smoke billowed across the plain.

For the beleaguered Jerries it must have seemed and sounded like Armageddon. For the battle-hardened troops on our side it was an unnerving experience. For young soldiers just arrived on the frontline it was a terrifying one. Some, on both sides, had little stomach for it and deserted, 'took a powder' as the saying went. During the frightful commotion I made periodic tours of our start lines to cheer the men up. I was furious to find two young soldiers cowering in their slit trench, clearly too afraid to move. 'Get out of there! Noise won't hurt you,' I yelled. They wouldn't budge, even when the CSM appeared at my side and threatened to shoot them. Poor devils, I thought later, having seen the effect of bombing and shelling on better men. Fortunately their behaviour wasn't copied by any of the Jocks in A Company, who went forward to the attack resolutely when the time came. Two were killed and seven wounded by mortar stonks as they sat waiting for H-hour (in army lingo, when the assault would start).

At H-hour minus ten minutes, Churchill tanks drove through our position to shoot up the enemy on the floodbanks. Wasp and Crocodile flame-throwers trundled up to within 25 metres of the near bank and blazed away at enemy dugouts. The banks of the Senio sizzled with flame and the air stank with petrol fumes. Oily black smoke billowed towards us. The armoured vehicles withdrew. Dozens of fighter-bombers streaked above our heads to strike further terror into the hearts of the enemy, making several low-level attacks with bombs and cannon, keeping Jerry heads down. They returned for a final run, a dummy one. Under its cover, the assault companies of the 8th Indian and 2nd New Zealand divisions launched their attack.

At 1920 hours we sprang from our trenches and sprinted forward through the flames, smoke and fading light. We knew we only had seconds to seize the Senio before the Germans sheltering in bunkers recovered from the bombardment and grabbed their weapons. Charges laid to blow a hole in the floodbank for us failed to explode, as the leads had been cut by shelling. In the event, that didn't matter. My men scrambled up and captured the near bank and flung a kapok bridge across the narrow trench of the river. Within minutes we were across and up and over the far bank and secured a bridgehead.

I saw one of my men have a miraculous escape. He trod on an S-mine which shot up in front of him and hung in the air. It failed to explode, to release its lethal ball bearings. The Jock collapsed in a dead faint. I glimpsed B Company and C Company yelling like dervishes, charging through the river, holding their rifles, Brens and tommy guns over their heads. Then, up and over the second bank, they disappeared into the twilight. D Company also passed through the position we had won. Assault pioneers followed to clear mines and tape safe paths beyond the river. Our eardrums were shattered and our nerves shaken by the whistle and roar of shells hurtling close overhead, a lifting barrage in front of B and C companies' advance. Flashes from the shell bursts pierced the smoke, picking out the now tiny figures of the Jocks darting here and there as they flushed out the Jerries. The horizon was lit by explosions and tracer as the other assaults went in all along the line.

Our bridgehead was now 500 metres beyond the Senio. At 2330 we linked up with the 6/13th whose men had crossed the river on our left. About midnight A Company was relieved by C Squadron, 6th Bengal Lancers, the division's reconnaissance regiment, and I led my men back into battalion reserve. The situation seemed confused but at Battalion HQ the mood was buoyant. The assault had gone according to plan. All along the line the German defences on the Senio had been breached in five minutes. By 0315 C and D companies had reached the Canale di Lugo, the night's objective, two kilometres from our starting point. By 0400 sappers had a Bailey bridge across the Senio near Fusignano, a bombed-out village on the far bank. I sat and watched tanks of A and C squadrons, North

Irish Horse rumble past to continue the advance, and then snatched a couple of hours of sleep.

At daybreak I was back on the far bank. Mist lay all around but the top of the floodbank was clear. This vantage point presented a surreal scene. The river banks smouldered from the previous night's fires and the air still carried the stench. The Senio was hidden in a trough of vapour. Gaping roofs at Fusignano appeared like a shipwreck on sea of fog. As it cleared I was amazed to see groups of Jerries emerging like rabbits from holes in the floodbanks, and I roused my exhausted men to round them up. Out of one deep dugout a platoon of shell-shocked soldiers appeared, their hands in the air, waving white rags. Numbed by our ferocious bombardment and assault the night before, and trapped in their bunkers while the battle raged above, they had evidently stayed hidden until morning. Knowing that Jerries with hands up to surrender often threw grenades in last acts of defiance (there had been just such an incident the night before), we took no chances. Some of my men were trigger-happy and showed it, so the Boche were very biddable. They were rounded up, glad to accept the fact that for them the war was over. Except for one German officer, an arrogant type with a sneer on his face who swaggered out with a disdainful glance at my men. I was very tempted to shoot him on the spot.

Despite the magnitude of the Battle of the Senio our casualties were light: two officers and eight other ranks killed, and two officers and 32 ORs wounded. Most of these were caused by mortar bombs and mines. Some were the result of friendly fire. After years of experience our aircraft-spotting was pretty accurate, so there was no mistaking the planes that attacked us at midday on the 10th. I watched in horror as American fighter-bombers dropped fragmentation bombs as we moved on the plain. We waved and cursed, to no effect. One of our men was killed and eight wounded including Padre Dow. The 6th Lancers and 3/15th Punjabis were hit also. I heard later that during the battle the Americans dropped fragmentation bombs on Polish troops killing over 100 men. The Poles were courageous soldiers whose contribution to the Allied cause is neglected. Yet theirs was the country we had gone to war for. McCreery had the decency to mention them in his message to the army before the battle.

After a week of rest and reorganisation behind the lines in peaceful countryside we went into action again. The Eighth Army was advancing to the Po. The Fifth Army had breached the Gothic Line at Monte Grande and swept down towards Bologna, which the Poles and partisans liberated on 21 April. The Argylls were ordered to Ferrara. At dawn on 20 April Brigadier Dobree set out in his Jeep, leading an advance party to recce Route 16, the Ravenna to Ferrara highway. The rest of the brigade followed during the day, passing through the Argenta gap, a hard-fought-for route above irrigated land deliberately flooded by the enemy. The smouldering wreckage of the German Tenth Army lay everywhere, hit by the fighter-bombers or discarded by demoralised troops as they retreated north. Not so demoralised though as to prevent some retaliation here and there, although they must have known it was all over for them. We were ambushed a few times by spandaus and SPs. Luck was everything, experience seemed irrelevant. CSM Carruthers, one of the battalion's most experienced men, a veteran of Sidi Barrani where he had won the Military Medal, was shot and killed by a sniper.

Ten kilometres short of Ferrara we stopped just forward of a 53rd Field Regiment battery, whose gunfire caused us an uneasy night. In the morning an order from Dobree came through: 'Get in and show the flag'. C and D companies, riding on tanks of the North Irish Horse, passed through a Punjabi forward line during the afternoon to seize bridges on a 50-metre-wide canal outside the city walls. Too late—the bridges had been blown. By early morning on 23 April the whole battalion was at the canal, with the 8th Argylls on our right. Patrols from C and D companies slipped across in assault boats at 0400. After sunrise A and B companies crossed by kapok bridges, and we got some Bren carriers, Jeeps, and motorbikes across by raft. A Bailey bridge and tanks would come later.

Partisans had seized Ferrara's biggest building, the formidable Estense Castle which commanded the city and the surrounding plain. They told us the centre was clear, and when we marched in we were mobbed by a cheering crowd in the main piazza. Lucky Jocks were handed wine and kissed by delirious girls, but the celebrations were premature. Shells whistled over and burst somewhere behind us. A and B companies fanned out into the streets when the partisans said they'd spotted some Jerries and Tiger tanks. We followed the guerillas as they ran forward to show us where. I got on the radio to Graham who ordered me to maintain our position, by then on the north perimeter, until he could get some tanks up in support. So we skulked around for the rest of the day keeping a lookout for counter-attacks.

The North Irish Horse turned up that evening and Jerry pulled out. We took 85 prisoners and captured several of the feared Tigers in working order. When I got back to the city centre I passed the Estense Castle and found Freddie Graham at a hotel, Albergo Annunziata, which he had commandeered for Battalion HQ. The Union Jack, the Stars and Stripes and the Italian flag flew above the entrance to the Palazzo Municipale. That ancient building, the ornate Duomo and the enormous Estense Castle made Ferrara seem a glorious prize and climax to our war. On the 27th the Pipes and Drums of 1st and 8th Argylls paraded in the piazza, watched by elated Ferrarese. They had seen the last of the goose-stepping Tedeschi. So had we. The war was about to end.

We reached the Po unopposed a few days later. It was an awesome sight. The wide river flowed with debris; embankments were strewn with the junk of the German army. Thousands of Jerries stranded without transport were captured, along with Italians, Czechs, Russians and other vagrants of war-torn Europe who had been conscripted by the Nazis as soldiers or labourers. The road and rail bridges were down, either bombed by our air forces or blown by Jerry. We climbed aboard amphibious APCs which gurgled and spluttered across. On 29 April we were ordered to stand-by for operations near Venice. To the disappointment of some bold-spirited fire-eaters thus deprived of the opportunity of being in at the kill, but to the relief of most of us, that order was cancelled. The honour of taking Venice went to the New Zealanders. We were content to settle into billets in and around Costa di Rovigo, a village 20 kilometres north of Ferrara.

On 2 May Field Marshal Alexander announced the unconditional surrender of the German forces in Italy. All across the plain, tracers and parachute flares were fired into the night sky in celebration—the last shots in the Eighth Army's war. Few know now of the achievements of 1st Battalion, the Argylls during its campaign from the Pyramids to the river Po . . . or that on that luminous plain in northern Italy one of the biggest and most successful Allied offensives of the Second World War took place.

After over four years of active service in all weathers and over all kinds of terrain, I rejoiced that it was over. We held an open-air thanksgiving and memorial service and thanked God, or our lucky stars, that we had survived. Our good fortune was tinged with sadness. We lost many comrades during the war: over 1,000 men from 1st Battalion were killed, wounded or missing. Yet most of us felt then, as I still do now, that we had played a part in a great crusade. We celebrated VE Day, 8 May 1945, in the piazza at Costa di Rovigo, where the Jocks of the Argylls and the Sepoys of the 6/13th Frontier Force Rifles indulged in exuberant merry-making around a huge bonfire that was lit in the middle of the square, to the delight of the local residents. Drink flowed freely, food was plentiful and Highland reels alternated with Indian war dances. I woke with a stunning hangover the next day, cured by the good news that I was to be posted home.

In his *History of the 1st Argylls 1939-1945*, Freddie Graham wrote what now must be considered an elegy for that evening of camaraderie at Costa di Rovigo and its era:

> The day that the 1st Battalion joined the 8th Indian Division was the first of many weary months of sustained fighting against a determined enemy . . . the battalion fought its way through snow and rainstorm, heat and mud, to the final victory in the fertile valley of the river Po. Across the rivers, over the towering peaks of the Apennines, through the fruit orchards and cornfields of the Po valley the war graves bear witness to the passage of the battalion. The spirit of comradeship and mutual admiration which grew up between the Indian fighting man and his British counterpart in the 8th Indian Division was one of the

reasons why the name of '8th Indian' was feared and respected even amongst the German paratroopers . . .

Like Freddie Graham, Brigadier Dobree wrote a heartfelt summary of his experience, in a parting message to 19 Brigade:

It is difficult for me to write in sufficient praise of the two Indian battalions. For not one single day of these testing years have either the 3/8th Punjab or the 6/13th Royal Frontier Force Rifles been anything but magnificent. They have displayed every soldierly quality in the highest degree: bravery, determination to win, coolness in battle, patience under the most adverse conditions, smartness when at rest and unfailing cheerfulness . . . The 1st Argyll & Sutherland Highlanders have lived up to the great traditions of their famous regiment and won a reputation for dash and tenacity which cannot be excelled . . . All of you, British and Indian officers and men of all tribes and classes have played your part unfailingly. You have more than upheld the highest traditions and spirit of the Indian Army. I cannot adequately express the pride I have felt in commanding the Brigade with three such battalions. As a Gunner and of the British service it has been the greatest honour that I ever have had or hope to achieve.

During our stay in Costa di Rovigo the Jocks were badgered into smartening themselves up; spit and polish, drill and training exercises. This was not to keep them happy (they were not amused) but to keep them on their toes and prevent them from becoming slack and stale, especially as the war against Japan had still to he won and the rumour was that we might be sent out to the Far East (in fact, the battalion soon returned to the UK). I didn't take much part in these goings-on. I had little enthusiasm for them and got my second-in-command and platoon commanders to do most of the work—delegation, the secret of command. Day trips to Venice were organised and I went on one, of which I recall only impressions: the drive on the causeway out into the dreamy lagoon; water taxis commandeered by Allied officers; the decaying palazzi and the Byzantine gloom of San Marco; the little orchestras in the Piazza. Freddie Graham offered me the command of the Guard of Honour to be formed by 1st Argylls and 6/13th Frontier Force Rifles for generals McCreery and Clark at a victory parade outside the Doge's Palace. I turned it down because I was impatient to leave Italy for home. I had arranged with Shaw—and MacDougall who was also being repatriated and had come over from his billet near Venice—to load a Jeep the CO had given us and drive to Naples where we would sail for Scotland.

So it was that on 11 May 1945, a hot sunny morning in northern Italy, I said goodbye to Sanders and the officers and men of A Company, assembled informally in front of me. I told them that they were a credit to the Argylls and that it had been my privilege to serve with them.

'Good luck to you all.'

Then one of the NCOs, an old hand from the desert days, stepped forward and called out: 'Three cheers for Major Ward!'

It was all over. I turned away. I never saw A Company again.

Jeep loaded, we set off on our route, visiting Lake Garda before heading south to cross the river Po, the Apennines and the remains of the Gothic Line. We stopped in Florence and drove through Tuscany and Umbria, camping each night in woody glades by the roadside and slept under the stars. No orders to obey, no inspections, or having to stand-to at dawn—a complete escape from military routine and discipline. Our only contact with the army was when we pulled into some depot or other to collect petrol and rations. In Rome we had a boozy lunch in the Borghese Gardens overlooking the city. Mac and Shaw had no desire to see Cassino again so instead of going inland we took the coast road to Naples, where we stayed at a hotel commandeered for officers' accommodation.

Apart from regretting that we couldn't keep the Jeep, I remember little about our embarkation. We didn't see the Rock of Gibraltar, as we passed through the strait at night, but I'll never forget the moment we saw the mountains of Argyll and anchored off Greenock on the Firth of Clyde. Mac, Shaw and I, soldiers three who had become friends at Stirling Castle as newly commissioned second lieutenants in December 1940 were home. I still had months to serve, at the Seaforth Highlanders' lonely barracks at Fort George on the shores of the Moray Firth before my release papers came through in 1946. Mac was more fortunate, being posted to the Highland Light Infantry barracks in Glasgow, as was Shaw who went to the Black Watch depot at Perth.

We disembarked at Greenock and took a train to Glasgow Central station where we parted, each with a month's leave. I was thrilled to see again familiar and fondly remembered streets and buildings and those beautiful clanging tramcars. My mother was still her usual cheerful, optimistic self, if older and more careworn than I remembered her. I was no longer the callow young man who had left home to join the Argylls in 1940. But I was alive and well, a little older and perhaps wiser. We spent a long time talking, exchanging news and stories, and I went to bed a tired and happy man. She was lucky: all her four sons returned safely from the war. She was with me on the morning of 27 September 1945 at Holyrood Palace in Edinburgh where I was decorated by His Majesty King George VI, with the Military Cross won at the Battle of Monte Cavallara. Two comrades, Major Walter Elder MC and Major Graham Wood MC, were also decorated by the king that morning. Photographs were taken as we strode through the grounds, wearing glengarries, kilts and badger-head sporrans. The local papers ran the pictures, copies of which I still have.

I went to London for an interview at the War Office, where I was offered a posting to the Allied Control Commission in Germany. I might have been posted to the sylvan setting of a village in the Bavarian Alps, but more likely I would have found myself is some blitzed or shell-shattered, poverty-stricken town in the Ruhr. Either that or a posting overseas, to bolster up the rapidly shrinking British empire. I declined. Freddie Graham, who stayed in the army, proposed a regular commission for me in the Argylls. I was flattered but turned it down. We kept in touch over the years, as I did with Mac, who went into HM Customs and Excise, joined a colonial police force, then returned to Islay, and Shaw who resumed his career in the law and settled in his home town of Oldham. Sanders went back to his job as the Bible Training Institute's caretaker in Glasgow where I visited him occasionally. Sergeant Bloomfield soldiered

on, becoming Drum Major, and I met him again at the Balaclava centenary event at Stirling Castle. Bill Dunn got a job as handyman to George
Orwell, then writing *Nineteen Eighty-Four*, on the Isle of Jura. I met him
there in 1947, while I was visiting family with Chris Mackay, my wife-to-
be, when he turned up at a ceilidh, complete with kilt and bagpipes.

After my hectic life on active service I found the peacetime environ-
ment was in some respects reassuringly familiar, in others disturbingly
altered. The problems of fitting into civvy street and deciding what to
do were difficult to solve. Some officers at Fort George had secure civilian jobs they looked forward to getting back to, but most of us had little
idea of what we would do in civvy street and were apprehensive about
the future. I rejoined my old firm of John Train and Company for a short
time then studied at Jordanhill College, qualifying as a teacher of primary
subjects and music at secondary level, and gained a diploma from the
Royal Academy of Music. I married, raised two sons, had modest success
as a singer and freelance writer and rose through the ranks of Glasgow
Corporation Education Department until I retired, a headmaster.

Around the time I retired, I attended an Argyll reunion. Among
those present was Major Rab Caldwell, whose capture by the Germans in
1944 led to my command of A Company. I hadn't seen Rab for 40 years,
although his frequent eccentric 'letters to the editor' of the *Glasgow Herald*
had assured me he was very much alive. There we sat, several recently
retired gentlemen, well-preserved and of modest means, strangers to each
other for so long, yet picking up our threads of talk as easily as a day-old
conversation. We left unspoken our thoughts of comrades killed in action.
We were the lucky ones. We were the survivors. Our awareness of that fact
tinged our recollections of well remembered incidents or half-forgotten
people and places with a kind of wistful cheerfulness. The years fell away
in a flash as we looked behind the outward appearance of our present age
and condition and saw in each other, as in glimpses of some previous
existence, the familiar faces, figures and personalities that had been ours
40 years before, as young men in uniform.

Those who served in the Second World War as infantrymen in

regiments with honourable traditions and proud histories belonged to a unique fellowship—comrades in arms who learned the meaning of esprit de corps. Most of us were just ordinary men of all types, cast in extraordinary roles and having to exist in extraordinary conditions. These may have brought out the worst in the few, but they brought out the best in the many. Wartime memories have never lain far under the surface of my mind, recollected clearly, often cherished in waking hours, or presenting their weird distortions in dreams and nightmares. By getting them off my chest I have, I hope, laid some ghosts to rest.

I was demobbed in April 1946, six years to the month after I joined the Argylls at Stirling Castle. At the clothing store where I was kitted out with civvies no distinction was made between officers and other ranks. Little deference and no favouritism was shown to officers. On the contrary, some of the fellows dishing out the clothes were bloody-minded enough to give us the shabbiest, most ill-made and ill-fitting garments. I got a nondescript suit, shirt, hat and other items which served me long enough till I could afford to buy better. I remember walking up Buchanan Street in Glasgow with Cecil, who had returned from the Far East and left the Marines by that time. In a moment of careless abandon, I threw my demob hat in the air and left it lying. A wee man came running up with it and said, 'You've dropped your hat, sir.'

'Keep it,' I told him. 'It's not a glengarry.'

Afterword

Ray Ward's memoir was found in an Afrika Korps ammunition box in the cellar of the family home in Glasgow after he died in 1999. The box was full of military memorabilia: papers, photographs, books, medals, and a diary written when he commanded General Montgomery's infantry bodyguard at El Alamein. I was fascinated by the diary and his narratives of the war in Italian East Africa, the Western Desert, the invasion of Sicily and the Italian campaign. His account of the Battle of Monte Cavallara when his leadership and courage were tested—what the Second World War soldier and poet Keith Douglas called 'the looking-glass which touches a man entering battle'—is crystal-clear.

His life was marked by the war and my brother Brian and I have been too by his experience of it. At our school, Jordanhill, in the 1960s the cadet corps was run by a major straight out of Dad's Army who, at the school show, would let boys aim (but not fire) a Bren gun and Lee Enfield rifles. Our school bags were army surplus haversacks. We played on local bomb sites. Comics we read and the films our father took us to see were about the war. Without irony they reiterated the moral certainties of his generation: the virtues of self-restraint, compassion, courage and honour.

Military-style discipline and ex-army eccentricities were common at home. His glengarry and sporran hung in the hall. For years he kept a pair of desert boots which were repaired until the suede perished. If we criticised his driving he'd say, 'What do you expect, I learned in the desert.' He never really talked about the war, to us or our mother, Chris Mackay, who was in the Auxiliary Territorial Service (ATS) at Dundonald camp in Ayrshire where, as she used to tell us, she typed out plans for D-Day. His postwar contact with the regiment was intermittent, motivated by bouts of nostalgia. He wrestled with the conundrum that war can bring out the best in women and men, and the enigma that he survived when so many of his comrades fell. For over 50 years, he was plagued by periodic flashbacks. We were woken often by his nightmares.

I read the memoir first as his son and later as an editor. He was an authoritarian figure, very much the company commander with emotions well camouflaged. Yet in the memoir he is an occasionally reckless, sensitive young man, which is how I see and know him now. After he was demobbed in 1946 he thought of emigrating to Canada. I asked him, after I relocated to Vancouver, why he didn't. He said he had travelled far, seen and suffered much and packed in enough experience to last a lifetime, during the war. He expressed no regrets at having been with the Argylls.

The contents of the Afrika Korps box helped fill gaps in his manuscript when I prepared it for publication, as did the *History of The Argyll and Sutherland Highlanders, 1st Battalion 1939-45* by Lieutenant-Colonel Graham, published in 1948. My father was sceptical of official accounts. As he put it, 'Official histories, written by senior commanders who may have had a troubled conscience about some incidents, and encounters so disturbing that they were sanitised or overlaid by a false or mistaken interpretation more acceptable to self-esteem, rarely tell the full story.' But he acknowledged a debt to his former commanding officer's book which was his aide-mémoire and became mine. Other primary sources were 1st Battalion's War Diary and the log of convoy No. WS5B, both held at The National Archives, Kew, and the battalion's wartime album at the Regimental Museum at Stirling Castle, to which I donated my father's desert diary and other papers as he would have done.

He and I talked of making a trip to his wartime places, but never got round to it. I made the trip for him in 2004 when I retraced 1st Battalion's route to the river Po. I drove north from Siena to Florence, through the 'deceptive Arcadia' of 1944. At Impruneta I had a vivid sense of déjà vu in the villa I rented—that he had been there. In the Apennines I crossed what had been the Gothic Line at Marradi, and saw Monte Cavallara. On Monte Cerere I found a memorial to the battle when the Argylls and Indian battalions beat off attacks by the German 1st Parachute Division. I stood and gazed on the Senio floodbanks that were stormed by the

Argylls in April 1945 and lingered in Ferrara, where Jocks dodged shells fired into the city by Tiger tanks. In Faenza, as I walked in the gloaming to my hotel on Corso Garibaldi, old-fashioned street lights flickered and I thought I saw a Jeep overtake me with three Eighth Army officers—Shaw, MacDougall and my father, who looked back.

My purpose was to find the men of A Company who died on Monte Cavallara. My father kept the casualty list. I had keyed the names into the Commonwealth War Graves Commission website, where I found the location of the graves, at Faenza. In the cemetery the headstones are identical. Each stone marks an individual serviceman. There is no hierarchy of race or rank, one of the CWGC's founding principles. There are British, Canadian, Indian, New Zealand and South African soldiers—1,152 in total at Faenza, one of the Commission's 123 burial grounds in Italy. I had a plan from the website to locate the 12 graves of A Company and found them all in row, as if on parade. I spotted Second Lieutenant Lindsay whose premonition was fulfilled. At Captain White's grave I crouched and touched the cold headstone's shoulder. I saw the date on the inscription and realised that it was almost 60 years to the day when those men died. White's inscription reads:

Remembered Always/Posterity Shall Know Thy Name

My father never forgot those names or that the years he had, his men who were killed were deprived of. I was alone in the cemetery and wondered what I would have done, and how I would greet the ghosts years later, had I been ordered to storm Monte Cavallara on 7 October 1944. My brother Brian and I will never step through that looking glass. Our generation has not been called upon to fight Fascist and Nazi tyranny, thanks to our fathers who did it for us.

Robin Ward
Edinburgh, Spring 2014